60 Feet, 6 Inches

AND OTHER
DISTANCES FROM HOME:
THE (BASEBALL) LIFE OF

Mose YellowHorse

Todd Fuller

Moses Yellowhorse
PITTSBURGH, N.L.

60 Feet, 6 Inches

AND OTHER DISTANCES FROM HOME: THE (BASEBALL) LIFE OF

Mose YellowHorse

Todd Fuller

HOLY COW! PRESS • DULUTH, MINNESOTA • 2002

Library of Congress Cataloging-in-Publication Data

Fuller, Todd, 1965—
60'6" and other distances from home: the (baseball) life of Mose YellowHorse.
p. cm.
ISBN 0-930100-76-X (paper)
(1. YellowHorse, Mose, 1898 - 1964. 2. Baseball players—United States—Biography.
3. Indian baseball players—Biography. 4. Pawnee Indians—Biography.)
I. Title.
GV865.Y45F85 2002
796.357/092 B 21   2002-17162

Holy Cow! Press books are distributed to the trade by Consortium Book Sales & Distribution, 1045 Westgate Drive, Saint Paul, Minnesota 55114. Our books are available through all library distributors and jobbers, and through most small press distributors, including Bookpeople, and Small Press Distribution. For personal orders or other information, write to: Holy Cow! Press, Post Office Box 3170, Mount Royal Station, Duluth, Minnesota 55803.

Acknowledgments

Grateful acknowledgment is made to *American Indian Culture and Research Journal, Crazyhorse, Puerto del Sol, Quarterly West, South Dakota Review,* and *Weber Studies,* in which some of this work first appeared.

I would also like to thank the Pawnee Nation for allowing me to conduct my field study in Pawnee in 1992, and for letting me return as needed. The people there who helped me are many, and they include Bob Chapman, President of the Pawnee Business Council (in 1992), Tom Knife Chief, Lois Knife Chief, and Dollie Gonzales, the Pawnee tribal librarian and archivist. Also those Pawnee elders and other tribal members who graciously shared their stories with me and taught me more about Pawnee culture and Mose YellowHorse's life than any historical study or journal article could have. I am indebted to them, especially Earl Chapman, Lawrence GoodFox, Phil Gover, Stacy Howell, John Jake, Albin LeadingFox, Anna Mulder, Nora Pratt, and Norman Rice, who have all passed away since my initial conversations with them. Their stories add texture, urgency, and humor to YellowHorse's story. Also, I am grateful to the Pawnee elders who continue on, including Maude Chisholm, Henry Stone Road, and Josephine Whish. Since 1992, I have met other tribal members who have shared their kindness by helping me see this book to its end; they include Mariah Gover (Phil Gover's granddaughter and my fellow graduate student at Oklahoma State University), Becky Eppler, who serves as Treasurer of the Pawnee Business Council, Debbie Echo-Hawk, head of the Pawnee Adult Education Center, and those others who offered encouragement—*choo-tha-kee.*

On a different note, I acknowledge the fact that the Pawnee tribal elders (and subsequently the Pawnee Nation, since some of those elders have passed on) who shared with me their Yellow-Horse stories are copyright holders of the oral narratives they told me and that I render in this text. It is only right that those individuals and the Pawnee Nation retain all the rights to those stories.

Other invaluable resources have been both the Endowment Association and the Creative Writing Committee at Wichita State University, whose generous grant awards allowed me to conduct my initial studies in Pawnee. Faculty members at Wichita State who encouraged me to pursue YellowHorse's story include Bruce Bond, Chris Brooks, Margaret Dawe, and Albert Goldbarth. The graduate students at Wichita State who shared their criticism and energy with me were Josh Friend, Carl Grindley, Corbet Hays, and Jennifer Cailin Oakes. All of their valuable insights continued to inform the work as it progressed.

At Oklahoma State University, where I continued my graduate studies in 1995, many people, faculty as well as students, helped me in my endeavors to reimagine YellowHorse's stories: I thank creative writing faculty members Lisa Lewis and Mark Cox and also offer a special thanks to Eric Anderson, whose guidance allowed me to embrace this project with rejuvenated enthusiasm. I also appreciate Sue Garzon's encouragement and insight. Among the students, I thank Monique Ferrell, Leslie Fife, Brad Gambill, Jennifer Hancock, Brad Hatley, Stuart Hoahwah, Grant Holt, Todd Petersen, Tony Spicer, Jubal Tiner, and Rod Zink. Their helpful comments in and out of workshops helped the progression of this project. I would also like to thank Steven L. Kite, a Ph.D. student in the Department of History at Oklahoma State, who proofread and shared with me his initial thoughts on this work. I appreciate too the comments and encouragement of other members of my dissertation committee, including L.G. Moses and Ed Walkiewicz.

I thank also photographer George Brace, Peter Clark of the Baseball Hall of Fame and Museum, Bill Conlin of the *Sacramento Bee*, D Jo Ferguson of *The Pawnee Chief*, John G. Hall, editor of *The KOM League Remembered*, Richard King at Drake University, Bob Lemke of *Sports Collectors Digest*, Mark Macrae, Sally O'Leary of the Pittsburgh Pirates, Jeff Powers-Beck at East Tennessee State University, and Carter Revard, Osage poet and teacher; also, the archival staffs at the *Arkansas Gazette*, Oklahoma Historical Society, *The*

Sporting News, and Tribune Media Services.

I give special thanks to Martha Royce Blaine, whose kindness and generosity helped me in the later stages of this project. Valuable information in her archival holdings, including field notes, tapes of dances, and pleasant conversations, allowed me to gain a fuller understanding of YellowHorse's life within the tribal community as a respected leader and keeper of the Pawnee culture.

I appreciate also the patience and encouragement of Jim Perlman, editor and publisher of Holy Cow! Press. From the moment he became involved in this endeavor, he understood both the importance of YellowHorse's life and the significance of the text's structure. His counsel and enthusiasm have allowed me to proceed with humility and excitement; I also thank Jan Zita Grover.

I extend thanks also to my parents, Dave and Cherye, whose guidance early on allowed me to recognize the beauty of both a well-timed curveball and those cultural differences within which we all live in the United States.

I am grateful to Natalie Peck, who never allowed me to give up on completing this work. Her editorial insights and critical commentary added texture and playfulness to the book.

TABLE OF CONTENTS

LIST OF ILLUSTRATIONS

*This book is dedicated to those members of the Pawnee Nation
of Oklahoma who helped me along the way—to those
who continue on in Pawnee and those who continue on elsewhere.
Their guidance, stories, and humor have made this endeavor
a most unexpected and rewarding journey.
I wish them and their families the best in all things.*

Death never ends feelings or relationships. . . . If a dear one passes on, the love continues and it continues in both directions—it is requited by the spirits. . . who send blessings back. . . . [so that] we have an idea or memory or concept of a person enduring long after the actual, physical person is gone. . . . [And] when someone dies, you don't "get over it" by forgetting; you "get over it" by remembering, and by remembering you are aware that no person is ever truly lost or gone. . . .
    —Leslie Marmon Silko, *The Legacy and Strength of Lace*

at times the heart looks toward open fields
and sees itself returning
    —Lance Henson, "near twelve mile point"

How does a human being know about these unseen powers? What is the source of this "religious feeling" . . . ? Many native people say it is the soul of a person who reaches out to touch the mysteries. Dreams and visions are born in the soul, and it is the soul that wonders about these things beyond the ordinary world.
    —Peggy V. Beck and Anna Lee Walters, *The Sacred*

First Meetings and Introductions

Finding Names

I FIRST MET MOSE YELLOWHORSE QUITE BY ACCIDENT, ONE EVENING IN THE fall of 1990.

At the time, I was bored at work, enduring another dull shift at my post with a financial printing company in Manhattan. I sought relief from both my duties and the recession by visiting numerous coworkers. I wandered from desk to desk, making small talk with those people who also seemed restless. We'd discuss the downward spiral of the Dow Jones average, the possibility of So-and-so's extra-marital affair, and always various sports-related issues. After half an hour of wandering through the office, I found myself talking baseball with a customer service rep who, I noticed, happened to have a copy of the *Baseball Encyclopedia* at his desk. I must've looked at the thing as if it were some kind of treasure: *anything* to pass the next three hours as quickly as possible. When he asked me if I wanted to borrow the book, I didn't hesitate.

Back at my desk, I flipped from one player's entry to the next: Ernie Banks, Fergie Jenkins, Ron Santo, Jim Thorpe, Billy Williams. I perused their various statistics as quickly as my eyes and fingers allowed: from Ted Williams to Babe Ruth to Grover Cleveland Alexander. And I was thankful to be working the third shift, away from bothersome high-salaried busybodies. Then, after an hour or so, as I was heading to Cy Young's entry, I saw the name *Chief Yel-lowhorse.* For two obvious reasons, I instantly assumed he was Native American. I then noticed that he was born and died in Pawnee, Oklahoma, which increased my hunch even more. I found other tidbits, too: his full name was Moses J. YellowHorse; he had been born on January 28 (the day after my own birth date), in 1898; he stood 5' 10" and weighed 180 pounds. I then examined his career totals:

YEAR	TEAM	W	L	PCT	ERA	G	GS	CG	IP	H	BB	SO
1921	PIT N	5	3	.625	2.98	10	4	1	48.1	45	13	19
1922		3	1	.750	4.52	28	5	2	77.2	92	20	24
2 YRS.		8	4	.667	3.93	38	9	3	126	137	33	43

And I immediately became engaged in fantasy: what he might've looked like; what his childhood might've been like in Pawnee; what great players he might've played with, or against. I became curious about his eight wins and four losses—which teams he defeated and which ones he lost to, which pitchers he dueled against, which great hitters he faced.

In short, I was intrigued by YellowHorse because he was Indian, played baseball, and did so at a volatile time in both the game's and the country's history. I then began contemplating the tensions inherent in a cultural equation that included an Indian throwing a baseball at (mostly) white batters, and the empowerment implied by such an action. In the same vein, I considered the visual and metaphoric resonance of the ball's colors; I also wondered about issues involving family and home.

Not five minutes after I saw his entry, I started writing. I began a piece in which I argued for his induction in the Baseball Hall of Fame, another about his playing days in Pittsburgh, and still another about his life in Pawnee after his baseball days ended. Though I knew none of the details of his life, I was too enthralled by my imaginings to care about specifics.

A Brief Explanation

When I came across YellowHorse's entry, it fired in me a curiosity that had come naturally since I was a kid. The reason I stopped at and became so intrigued by his entry can be explained by his name, YellowHorse, and the fact that I came upon it in the *Baseball Encyclopedia*. This specific combination of an Indian and a baseball player brought together two facets of American culture that had always intrigued me. Ever since I was forced to read Indiana history in fourth grade, I wanted to learn more about the Indians against whom the whites fought. For some reason, I empathized with the numerous tribes who were dislocated from their lands, way of life, and cultures. I learned that various Indian groups were able to survive repeated Euroamerican attempts to destroy them, and their survival seemed to me a good thing. In my *Dick-and-Jane* understanding of American history, it seemed to me that great wrongs had been committed repeatedly against Indians. The way my teacher told it, all the land in America had belonged to many different Indian tribes. But as a result of wars, broken promises, and disease, Indians were forced off their lands or lied to about their treaties with the U. S. government, or died from infectious diseases they caught from whites. She always managed to convey this information to us in a tone that suggested wrongdoing by white settlers and politicians. Though I always remained intrigued by things Native American and even read quite a lot about various tribes, my understanding barely reached beyond a 1950s Hollywood Indian stereotype.

While developing this intellectual and emotional curiosity about Indians in the mid-70s, I was at the same time failing, year after year, to become a baseball star. I could never manage to put aside my fear of a hard spherical object traveling at me—either off an opponent's bat or from a pitcher's hand. So, while I eventually admitted my fears (to myself) and quit playing Little League, I always enjoyed studying and learning about the game's nuances. I received most of that baseball knowledge by watching Chicago Cubs' broadcasts on WGN and listening to Jack Brickhouse's play-by-play. By an unfortunate curse of birthright, I am a Cubs fan (and remain one to this day) and spent many summer afternoons discovering the likes of Manny Trillo, Bill Madlock, and Fergie Jenkins. These broadcasts nurtured in me an admiration for a game that I could not and would not play. I'd always watch in awe as some fielder snared a ball in midflight, as a pitcher delivered a breaking curveball, as a batter sent a pitch into the left field bleachers. Beyond the physical, I enjoyed also cerebral aspects of the game: the cat-and-mouse between a would-be base stealer and the pitcher; the chess-like moves between managers—when to bring in a relief pitcher, whom to call on in a pinch-hitting situation, when to make defensive substitutions. All these aspects of the game captured my attention. Even now, as I endure one Cubs' baseball season after another, I peruse box scores daily and watch as many games as time allows.

Taken together, then, my curiosity about both Indians and baseball started at a young age. And that night in 1990 when I sat in my office flipping through the *Baseball Encyclopedia* and saw Chief YellowHorse's entry, my two interests intersected. I knew of other Indian ballplayers like Thorpe, Charles Bender, and Allie Reynolds. But for some reason, the names *YellowHorse* and *Pawnee, Oklahoma,* ignited my imagination differently. It seemed one of those moments when something so unexpected instantly became something perfect, serendipitous. Because of this, I reacted in many ways as a fourth grader, with wonder and delight. During the weeks and months that followed, I continued to write about YellowHorse, using mostly information contained in his entry.

The Ol' Unexpected Epitaph

Unfortunately, at twenty-five and with a full-time job, I didn't have the resources necessary to conduct a major research project, especially about someone who lived and died halfway across the country. Within the span of a year, however, I moved from New York to Wichita, Kansas, to begin a master's degree, and I quickly realized my close proximity to Pawnee. After settling in and becoming comfortable with Wichita, I started entertaining notions of a road trip south. The right time for that journey occurred on a warm and sunny Sunday in March 1992.

As I made my way toward Oklahoma and Pawnee for the first time, I noticed changes in the landscape—the flat prairie with its many wheat fields gave way to the foothills of the Ozarks, the "green country" in the northeastern quadrant of the state. I was also aware of my entering the old Indian Territory, where the government under numerous administrations had relocated many tribes. Because of this, I drove with an intense alertness, my eyes fixed more on signs and the land's textural features than on the road. For some reason, I was half-hoping, half-expecting to come across one of those historical markers when I arrived in Pawnee—something that acknowledged Moses YellowHorse's playing days in the majors. What I encountered as I approached the western outskirts of town, however, was a large brown sign for Pawnee Bill's Mansion, whoever Pawnee Bill was. And not a minute later, as I neared the town square, I saw another surprising image—a huge Dick Tracy mural painted on the side of a bank building. At the bottom of the mural, I read

Chester Gould
Birthplace 1900
Pawnee Oklahoma

and mumbled "I'll be damned." After taking a picture of the mural, I continued to look for some acknowledgment of YellowHorse; I drove through the town square, saw a number of war memorials to Pawnee's veterans, but came up empty in my attempt to locate the name YellowHorse on any kind of historical memento. Feeling both a little frustrated and puzzled, I finally went to the police station, the least desirable option for gathering general information, in my view. Two uniformed officers told me I could find his headstone at the North Indian Cemetery and gave me directions: "North on 18, 'bout half a mile outside of town." They also informed me that they didn't know of any tribute, either in town or on the tribal grounds.

The drive to the North Indian Cemetery took all of five minutes, and once there I was intrigued to find two graveyards—one for the Indian dead, the other for whites—with a row of twenty cedars separating them. The Pawnee side of the cemetery lay to the north, the white side to the south, each on a hill that sloped upward to the north. Among hundreds of stones from the 1870s on, I saw pictures of couples in traditional Pawnee clothes, noticed various family plots—the Govers, Echo-Hawks, Lone Chiefs—and stopped at many veterans' headstones. Still, I wandered from stone to stone hoping to find "YellowHorse" with each glance, and I became more determined with each "Knife Chief" and "GoodFox" that I read. After half an hour of searching, I started wondering whether or not the police officers were having a laugh at my expense. Then, in one of those Murphy's-Law-like moments, I finally spotted a headstone located at the extreme southwestern corner of the Indian Cemetery. A small gray stone stood isolated from all the rest, closer to the white cemetery than any of the others. As I walked quickly toward it, I started making out the letters in YellowHorse's name, and I started jogging for some reason. When I looked down to read the inscription, I saw something I never expected or anticipated:

MOSE YELLOWHORSE
1898–1964
FIRST FULLBLOOD INDIAN IN
MAJOR LEAGUES
PITTSBURGH PIRATES 1921-22

And I stood stunned again, same as I had been when I first came upon his entry in the *Baseball Encyclopedia*. A myriad of thoughts fired through my head: *Is this true? That's right, Jim Thorpe wasn't full-blooded. Wasn't Bender full-blooded? Weren't there other players before the 1920s? YellowHorse, really?* And again, for the second time during my first visit to Pawnee, I said to myself, "I'll be damned."[1]

Research and Ramifications

Finding this information when and where I did—that is, right at the beginning of my research and in a cemetery—remains seminal to the evolution of this project. It allowed me to realize, even dream about, the possibilities of encountering the unexpected at any moment. I realized also how important it might be to write a book about Mose YellowHorse, if nothing significant had been written already. So as soon as I returned to Wichita, I went to the library and started searching through databases and card catalogs: no full-length study devoted to YellowHorse had been published. I looked in baseball- and Native American-related texts for his name: the most I found was a brief blurb in *The Who's Who of Baseball*. And in the span of a few short hours that carried me from standing in front of YellowHorse's stone to searching through books and databases for his name, the seeds of a project had been planted and begun to sprout.

Within the next few weeks my efforts to locate something full-length and substantial—even an article—turned up nothing. Shortly after, I started writing grant proposals and letters to the Pawnee Nation of Oklahoma. I spoke on the phone to numerous people associated in one way or another with baseball, Oklahoma history, or Pawnee history. Again and again, my colleagues at Wichita State encouraged me to pursue the project with all my attention. And finally, in June 1992, my Toyota Tercel packed with pens, paper, a typewriter, and other provisions, I headed south to Pawnee again—this time, with a mind to listening to stories about YellowHorse's life.

Though some tribal members were a bit reluctant at first to talk with me, I returned every day until I began hearing stories about YellowHorse's life. (That's when I learned the proper spelling of his name.) The initial conversations I had with tribal members inspired the text that follows, much of the poetry, and information in the essays. Had I not listened to and incorporated their many stories, the text would not have become the community-like collaboration it is, an effort to share as many perspectives as possible: I heard the one about YellowHorse's arm getting strong by first tossing rocks in an attempt to capture small game; I listened to stories about his fastball, said to be as quick as Walter Johnson's. Anna Mulder told me about YellowHorse's beautiful whistle, which she could hear as he approached her house; Earl Chapman shared that YellowHorse went fishing at his favorite spot just five days before he died. These stories and many others energize the text, adding humor and lending a dimension to YellowHorse's life and character that would be lacking otherwise.

Having the opportunity to listen to so many stories and anecdotes about YellowHorse's life allowed me to understand his
continuing importance in the Pawnee community: his accomplishments, both as a ballplayer and a tribal elder, still make many tribal
members proud. Over the course of more than a decade since I first
read YellowHorse's name in the *Baseball Encyclopedia*, I have
encountered numerous people, both young and old, who smiled
when they shared their YellowHorse stories with me. Given this, I
realized that I was extremely fortunate to be learning about a man
who seemed to make so many people happy. And as I gathered
newspaper stories, box scores (from his major and minor league
days, even his school days), as I listened to and read stories about
his professional and personal feats, I realized that YellowHorse
kept his own dignity intact as he crossed cultural boundaries to
play in major league baseball—the most sacred of (white) American games.

Within a Larger Context

By the time YellowHorse advanced to the major leagues, earning a spot on the Pirates' 1921 roster, any number of Indian players
had seen action at the highest level of professional baseball.
Though a complete list is nearly impossible, some of these players
included Charles Bender (Ojibwa), Jim Bluejacket (Cherokee),
George Johnson (Winnebago), John Meyers (Cahuilla), Billy Phyle
(Lakota), Louis Sockalexis (Penobscot), Ed Summers (Kickapoo),
Jim Thorpe (Sac and Fox), and Ben Tincup (Cherokee). Of these
nine players, Bender and Thorpe achieved the most fame—Bender
as a pitching ace for Connie Mack's Philadelphia Athletics and
Thorpe as an Olympian and football player. John Meyers, who
played catcher for nine years, mostly with John McGraw's New
York Giants, also enjoyed a successful major league career. Nearly
fifty years after his playing days were over, Meyers elaborated on
his experience as an Indian ballplayer, stating, "In those days,
[1909-1917] when I was young, I was considered a foreigner. I didn't

belong. I was an Indian" (Ritter 172). Such a statement clearly suggests that Meyers (as well as other Indian players?) was not always welcome on the playing field or in his own team's clubhouse. (It goes without saying that an Indian securing a roster spot meant one less job for a white ballplayer, and the idea of an *ethnic* player "taking" employment away from a Euroamerican did not always sit well with other players or fans. One need only remember the well-documented struggles faced by the likes of Hank Greenberg and Jackie Robinson to contextualize the difficulties Indians endured much earlier.) Taken together, this notion of being an outsider and unwelcome created an unpleasant situation for many Indian ballplayers.

A quick survey of newspaper stories about Indian players suggests that many writers (in major and minor league cities) from the turn of the twentieth century on employed stereotypic depictions of Indian players. Sports writers often resorted to images of Indians as noble or savage; they sometimes used language suggesting that most players (or teams, in the case of the Cleveland Indians) were nineteenth-century plains warriors. Most Indian players were portrayed by the media inaccurately, with arcane images. One example, which appeared in the *Pittsburgh Gazette* in 1921, involved a physical description of YellowHorse and described the pitcher as being "as dark as the previous night's lunar eclipse."[2] This obvious reference to YellowHorse's skin color suggests a comparative connection between the pitcher and nature—that mysterious attribute that all Indians (supposedly) possess in their relationship with the physical landscape—while at the same time freely offering a suspicious observation that the Pawnee pitcher was *darker* than the average major leaguer. In another example, Harry A. Williams, a writer for the *Los Angeles Daily Times*, invoked a more romantic stereotype in his April 1916 account of a difficult game that George Johnson endured:

Seals Scalp Chief Johnson
Washington Park was made uninhabitable for Indians yesterday. The Seals chased Chief Johnson to the underbrush in less than

one round and later in the game a long foul went into the right field bleachers and almost hit a Washoe buck who came all the way from Inyo county on horseback to root for the Chief. The noble red man from Inyo then left the park, complaining that the white settlers had made this an unsafe place in which to live.[3]

Here, the suggestion of white domination over Indians is so obvious as to allege that Johnson and his fellow Indian guest are completely out of place in a contemporary (American) setting. In another example, an unidentified headline writer for the *Sacramento Bee* wrote of YellowHorse, who spent the 1923 season with the Sacramento Solons, that "Pawnee Mose, Aided By Fifty Plains Pals, Puts Indian Sign On Tigers." The text goes on to state:

Fifty Indians, who have been showing at a local theater, danced around the home plate at Washington Park and hung the Indian sign on the Tigers, and Moses Yellowhorse won the first game of the doubleheader, 5 to 2. There were no Indians around for the second game and Vernon grabbed it 2 to 1.

As these examples demonstrate, Indian ballplayers often found themselves in a representational time warp that confined their identities within a specific lexicon of images and activities: the brave, the warrior, the savage, the noble red man, and that most popular of monikers—the Chief; likewise, players were busy scalping (or being scalped), placing curses (or being cursed), beating the warpath (or being beaten on the warpath), tracking an enemy (or being tracked), etc.

Writers often discussed players' physicality in terms reminiscent of romantic notions associated with the noble/savage Indian. Depicting Indians in such a manner dates as far back as Columbus, who described the Carib as being "very well built, with very handsome bodies and very good faces," and went on to say in the same journal entry that they were "generally fairly tall, good looking and well proportioned."[4] Over four centuries later, writers employed similar descriptions and language when talking about Indian players like John Meyers, George Johnson, and even YellowHorse. At one time or another, all were described as "great physical specimens," as being "well-built," and "quite good looking." Joe Vila wrote of YellowHorse in the spring of 1921 that "the redskin should prove a splendid investment" and that he was "strongly built."[5] As Ward Churchill, Norbert S. Hill, Jr., and Mary Jo Barlow observe in "An Historical Overview of Twentieth Century Native American Athletics,"

> The Native American within non-Indian mythology is (and always has been) an overwhelmingly physical creature. [To this end,] sport was and is an expedient means of processing this physicality into a "socially acceptable" package without disrupting mythology; Indians tracked as "Indians" into the mainstream. There could be but one result of such manipulation: dehumanization of the Native Americans directly involved and, by extension, dehumanization of the nonparticipating Native Americans whom the athletes represented in the public consciousness. Thus the myth of the American savage was updated, abut essentially unchanged. (31)

Perpetuating such fantasies served to reach "a public satisfied with wooden Indians rather than living, breathing human beings" (31). Of course, there exists within the context of this situation a confounding variable—that sports writers met and spoke with Indian ballplayers, which allows for the probability that many writers did in fact know them as living, breathing human beings. Given this, it becomes clear that the media consciously chose to portray Indian players inaccurately.

And on the Other Side of the Coin

Though it is true that many writers misrepresented Indian ballplayers, which did nothing to enhance those players' experiences, it is true also that someone like YellowHorse was well-liked by teammates and fans. Despite the fact that writers often depicted him in racist ways, character traits identified by writers, players, and Pawnee tribal members that may have contributed to YellowHorse's popularity were his sense of humor and his even-handed sense of kindness. With regard to the first, numerous accounts speak to YellowHorse's quick wit and willingness to play jokes. Longtime sports writer Frank Lieb said that YellowHorse had "a sense of southwestern humor that reminded listeners of the late Will Rogers, who was also of part Indian extraction" (192). Another example, a retrospective, occurs in the July 6, 1973 edition of *Steel City Sports;* the title reads "YellowHorse: Indian With a Funny Bone," and then delves into several shenanigans that YellowHorse pulled with teammate Walter "Rabbit" Maranville. Years after Yel-lowHorse's playing days had ended, teams he'd played for in Pittsburgh, Little Rock, and Sacramento held tributes in his honor. A noted tribute occurred in January 1964, just months before Yel-lowHorse died, when Sam Gordon, owner of the Sacramento team, held a celebration for his former pitcher. A story from *The Sacramento Union,* "Indian Star Back Home for Gordon," went so far as to state that YellowHorse was "one of [Sacramento's] all-time colorful sports figures."[6]

Other notable tributes to YellowHorse included a lifetime pass to the World Series given to him by the Pirates, their donation of his glove to the Baseball Hall of Fame and Museum in 1958 (where it remains on display), and the Pirates fans' chanting, "Bring in Yel-lowHorse!" when they wanted a dependable reliever to enter the game. That such a chant evolved at all seems an interesting point, the fans' grateful acknowledgment of his professionalism; this for a pitcher who only played in thirty-eight games. Had the chant endured for a year or two after YellowHorse's departure, it might not be so surprising, but the fact is, Pirates' fans continued to yell the chant more than twenty-five years after YellowHorse last pitched for the organization. I doubt that any other player, who played such a brief time, ever received this kind of fan tribute. Given this, and the number of good-natured stories told about Yel-lowHorse, it is fairly easy to determine that he was well-liked by many of the fans and players with whom he was associated during his professional career.

To this end, Pawnee tribal member Earl Chapman said of YellowHorse's experiences in Pittsburgh that "the owners, players,
fans . . . all treated him with respect . . . [and] that Mose was always
quick to make friends. That was the kind of man he was, no matter
where he went." Other tribal members also echo a similar sentiment, saying that he was quick to laugh, humble, and made friends
easily. Such attributes would explain YellowHorse's popularity in
Pittsburgh, Sacramento, even Little Rock, and especially Pawnee.
It's no surprise, then, to find that after posting an impressive victory for the Pirates, YellowHorse was described as "the latest idol of
the Smoky city fans."[7]

Because of all this, it might be that YellowHorse's experience in
professional baseball was the so-called "exception to the rule" with
regard to the representation and treatment of most Indian ballplayers. Certainly George Johnson and John Meyers found the going
rough at times. Bender, for his part, stated to a *Chicago Daily News*
reporter in 1910 that "[T]here has been scarcely a trace of sentiment
against me on account of birth. I have been treated the same as
other men."[8] This clearly suggests that Bender's experience could
have been more positive than negative. Stephen I. Thompson
notes, however, that "the interview in question occurred while
Bender was still an active player, negotiating annual contracts and
living from day to day with teammates and opponents who presumably read the newspapers" (4). The implication being that
Bender didn't want to say anything that might be detrimental to
his career. Of course, Bender lived until 1954 (almost thirty years
after he quit playing) and never contradicted his earlier statement,
as best as I can tell. I would imagine that other players, though
they endured a perpetuation of media stereotyping, also found
their playing days satisfying on a number of levels.

YellowHorse Versus the Past

In 1921 accounts about YellowHorse's breaking into the major
leagues, writers' comparisons between him and Bender seem
forced and inevitable. At least two writers, Norman E. Brown and

Joe Vila, both stated that YellowHorse might well be a newer ver-
sion of Charles Bender. Brown wrote, "It's a good bet that [Pirates'
manager George Gibson] 'll keep the new Chief Bender."[9] Part of the
headline in Vila's story reads, "Pirates Hope That Newest Redskin
Recruit to Baseball Will Become a Second Bender." That writers
would be attracted to the easy comparison of two Indian pitchers is
not startling, and Bender was the most successful Indian pitcher,
with 210 wins. But other Indian ballplayers achieved notable major
league careers: Ed Summers, who pitched for Detroit from 1908 to
1912, achieved a career pitching mark of 68 wins and 45 losses;
John Meyers caught in 925 games, batted .291 during his career,
.358 in 1912 (and .357 during that year's World Series), and col-
lected 826 hits; George Johnson won 41 games in three years;
Sockalexis had a lifetime batting average of .313; and Thorpe hit
.327 in his last year in the majors (1919) before embarking on his
professional football career, which would eventually earn him a
spot in the Pro Football Hall of Fame.

Of all these major leaguers, Bender and Meyers certainly sustained the most successful careers. Even among this list of Indian
ballplayers, YellowHorse's professional totals are modest. When
one considers, however, that he won 54 games and lost 28 (a clip of
66%) over the span of his professional career (mostly with Little
Rock of the Southern Association and Sacramento of the Pacific
Association), then it's obvious that his major league appearance was
well-deserved. The velocity of his fastball helped him to pitch successfully through numerous ailments. It also kept him in semipro
circles in Oklahoma until 1940. That he would pitch competitively
after his fortieth birthday, even with an arm that caused him problems, is a testament to his desire to play baseball. It explains,
perhaps, the multitude of stories about his endurance and athletic
skills. In fact, when I first started listening to stories about his
pitching and his career, tribal members often told me that he
struck out Babe Ruth in some barnstorming game. I discovered a
full account of the narrative in 1995 when Darrell Gambill, head of
the Pawnee Chamber of Commerce, wrote about it in *The Pawnee*

Chief. He stated,

> It was October 2, 1922 and a great day for baseball in Drumright [Oklahoma]. . . . [And] Babe Ruth would be on the Drumright team.

The story continues:

> The fans roared as Ruth came to bat in the first inning. . . . 4 pitches whistled across the plate. The Babe missed three of them and struck out. The crowd sat in silence.

Then in the third inning,

> He took a wicked swing at the first pitch and missed. He let a low outside pitch go by. Then he stepped up and took a vicious cut at the third pitch for strike 2. A low inside pitch brought the count to 2-2. The next pitch was sizzler down the middle. [Ruth] didn't come close. . . . There was no joy in Drumright that day. The mighty Bambino had struck out with the bases loaded. Drumright lost to Shamrock 7-5.

The story then concludes:

> The fans knew the pitcher playing with Shamrock was . . . Pittsburgh Pirate . . . Moses YellowHorse. . . .[10]

Stories like this demonstrate that YellowHorse possessed the big-league skills necessary to compete, even thrive. Unfortunately, a series of injuries and poorly-timed late nights prevented YellowHorse from achieving his place alongside Bender. First, an injury in 1921 sidelined him for half the season, and then he sustained permanent arm damage at the beginning of the 1924 campaign when he entered a game for Sacramento without warming up adequately.

Within this context, then, YellowHorse distinguished himself in several ways as an Indian in major league baseball: first, his fastball traveled in the mid-90s; second, he earned the friendship and respect of players associated with the Pirates' organization; third, he received several lasting tributes from people who saw him play; fourth, he earned a reputation as both a fun-loving and smart player, always quick to laugh, always eager to learn about the art of pitching; finally, he had, in each of his seasons as a professional, a winning percentage (aside from the injury-filled season in 1924, when he went 1-4). Given these factors, I found it somewhat surprising that no one had recorded aspects of his career and life much earlier, while he was still alive.

Why All the Effort? And Other Closing Thoughts

YellowHorse's story, like that of other Indian ballplayers, touches on aspects of American culture and history, including assimilation, identity, and survival. Like other players before him, YellowHorse faced media that often misrepresented him through stereotypes and inaccurate images; in opposing cities, he heard the taunts of fans and players. Because of these and various other reasons, all former Indian major leaguers' stories are worth examining. Indian ballplayers faced different challenges than their white teammates and opponents. As a result, their major league experiences were not, and are not, the same as most white players'.

In YellowHorse's case, he was able to use his skills to earn a living, and he made many friends in the process. After his playing days concluded, he was able to work through personal problems, begin life renewed in the mid-1940s, and become a respected tribal leader. While he played baseball, he played as a team member, but he never lost sight of his Pawnee identity. When he returned to Pawnee, he achieved a local celebrity status and became involved in tribal matters. A body of stories and anecdotes about the many aspects of his life developed since then. People in the Pawnee communities (Indian and non-Indian) continue to tell stories about him, more than thirty-five years after he passed away, a vibrant testament to his importance in those communities. He is a source of pride to many people, and it seems to me that such a man is worthy of close examination.

. . .

Much of the work that follows examines, scrutinizes, imagines, and celebrates various aspects of YellowHorse's life. It is not attempting to be an exhaustive "Western" study; rather it is a literary biography that includes poetry, oral narratives, some fiction, creative nonfiction, and critical essays. I have incorporated newspaper stories, tribal documents, cartoons, photographs, and transcripts. I have developed the text in this manner in the hope of creating both a community collaboration and a kind of old-time Pawnee storytelling session in which many voices have their say about YellowHorse's life. This means that tribal members, photographers, illustrators, other writers (Indians and non-Indians), other ballplayers, even *Dick Tracy's* late creator, Chester Gould, and I take turns offering perspectives on YellowHorse as an Indian, a baseball pitcher, a troubled man, a respected tribal leader, and a celebrated figure.

. . .

Notes

1   Since beginning my work on this project, I spent numerous hours attempting to verify the validity of this claim. At various turns along the way, I felt confident that YellowHorse was, in fact, the first full-blooded Indian in the major leagues. A number of sources, including journal articles, newspaper stories, not to mention the many Pawnee tribal members' stories seemed to confirm such a claim.

In an article titled "Moses YellowHorse: The Tragic Career of a Pittsburgh Pirate," *Pittsburgh History* Winter 1995/96: 186-89, William Jakub states near the beginning of his essay that YellowHorse was "the first 'full-blooded' Indian to play major league baseball."

A story, "Indian Star Back Home for Gordon," published by *The Sacramento Union* in its January 20, 1964 edition finds that "He [YellowHorse] was the first full-blooded Indian to play in the major leagues."

Also, a number of YellowHorse's obituaries affirm this assertion. For one, the *Stillwater News Press*, published in Oklahoma, stated that "Chief Yellowhorse [sic] was said to be the first full-blood American Indian to play baseball in the major leagues;" *The Sporting News* obituary asserted that "Moses (Chief) YellowHorse, [was] one of the few full-blooded Indians who reached the majors;" the Associated Press's obituary said "Moses YellowHorse . . . claimed to be the first full-blooded Indian to have played major league baseball."

Even with all this, some scholars have more recently questioned whether or not YellowHorse, or Louis Sockalexis (a Penobscot outfielder who played with Cleveland from 1897-99), or Ben Tincup (a Cherokee pitcher who broke in with the Phillies in 1914) might have been the first full-blooded Indians to play in the majors. As Tim Wiles, a researcher at the Baseball Hall of Fame and Museum, told me, however, "I don't think there's any way to determine . . . who is the earliest Native American full-blooded major league baseball player."

For his part, baseball scholar Joseph Giovannetti (Tolowa) suggested his skepticism about Sockalexis's full-blood quantum when he stated to me that "He [Sockalexis] appears between 3/4 and full-blood."

Given all this speculation, it seems nearly impossible to determine exactly, without question, who might have been the first full-blooded Indian in the majors. Certainly, many people, including Pawnee tribal members, scholars and journalists in different parts of the country, and non-Indians in Pawnee, believe YellowHorse earned the right to claim such an assertion. Given my biases, I am inclined to agree. Since my goal in this text is to examine and celebrate YellowHorse's life and career through various filters and perspectives and since this is a creative text, I am not attempting to offer the last word on this situation. The issues of first-ness and full-blooded-ness are both extremely political in their different ways, and I hope that other scholars might one day answer these questions more fully—if such a thing is possible or even necessary.

2 As quoted in William Jakub's article "Moses YellowHorse: The Tragic Career of a Pittsburgh Pirate." Jakub does not attribute the quotation to anyone.

3 Harry A. Williams, "Seals Scalp Chief Johnson," *Los Angeles Daily Times* 27 Mar. 1916.

4 "Pawnee Mose, Aided by Fifty Plains Pals, Puts Indian Sign on Tigers," *Sacramento Bee* 30 Apr. 1923.

5 Columbus, Christopher. "The Indians Discover Columbus" in *The Journal of Christopher Columbus*. Ed. L. A. Vigernas. (London: Orion, 1960): 23-24.

6 "Indian Star Back Home for Gordon," *The Sacramento Union* 20 Jan. 1964.

7 "Pirates Winners after Long Battle," *New York Times* 17 June 1921: "Yellowhorse, the latest idol of the Smoky City fans, relieved Adams in the fourteenth and turned the Robins [Brooklyn Dodgers] back with even regularity."

8 As quoted in Stephen I. Thompson's "The American Indian in the Major Leagues," *The Baseball Research Journal* (1983): 1-7.

9 Norman E. Brown, "Starring in Sports: Moses Yellowhorse," 1921.

10 Darrell Gambill, "Pawnee: Town & Country," *The Pawnee Chief* 18 Jan. 1995.

Some Numbers

Courtesy of D Jo Ferguson

One writer described YellowHorse rather insensitively, as being "as dark as the previous night's lunar eclipse." But Mose YellowHorse, as this photograph shows, possessed an intensity in his eyes that was mesmerizing.

Memorizing Oklahoma:
A Chant (in 1992) that Includes the Word First

These are my first steps into the cemetery,
And I'm concentrating on the names chiseled
Into hundreds of granite headstones. None

Of the ghosts of my relatives has called me
Here. But I'm captivated by names like
Echo-Hawk and Lone Chief. I'm wide-eyed

By the row of twenty cedars that separates
The Indian dead from the white. And I will
Pause at some of the graves to consider

The mounted photos of men and women in
Traditional Pawnee dress: the dead always
Know when we're looking. They can feel

The weight of our bodies above them.
And with my first steps into Oklahoma, I'm
Beginning to wonder if I'll ever find a man

Named YellowHorse. I'm starting to wonder
If I should retreat to my Toyota, to the road,
Then two hours north to Kansas, where it's

Easy to forget. I could say *It was just a Sunday
Drive.* I could tell myself *It was just another
Cemetery.* But this is one moment when I

Begin to hear the soliloquy of a fastball
Dividing the voices of a March wind. This
Is one time when the momentum of my

Curiosity will not rest. And soon enough
I'll sit in front of a stone marked MOSE
YELLOWHORSE and repeat the lines

Of his epitaph for years to come: First Full
Blood Indian in / Major Leagues / Pittsburgh
Pirates 1921-22. Soon enough palominos

Will begin charging into my thoughts. I'll
Give myself the task of memorizing the red
Seams of a baseball. And I'll begin to dream

At all hours of the day in YellowHorse
Technicolor.

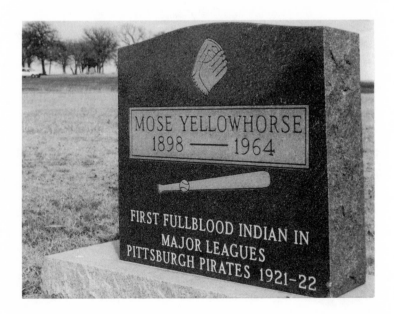

A Nonlinear Chronology

1921 On April 15, in Cincinnati: a baseball (just released from
      Mose YellowHorse's right hand) is a dancing red spine
      dividing the atmosphere in two.

      And it's his first pitch as a major leaguer. And all the boys
      yell "That's the way to fire it in there, Chief!"

      YellowHorse smiles at the sound of "Strike one."

1873 In August, a hunting party of some 1,000 Sioux meet a
      smaller Pawnee hunting party in southern Nebraska near
      the Republican River, and a fight ensues. Close to two hun-
      dred Pawnees lose their lives. The attackers burn the
      Pawnee bodies (including women and children) in a ravine.
      (But you didn't see that in *Dances with Wolves*.)

1901 With the Pawnee Bill Wild West Show, YellowHorse (at
      three) plays a "savage Indian boy" during a performance
      called *The Indians Attack*, in which a blood-thirsty band of
      crazed Indians mercilessly pillages a *peaceful* wagon train.
      While the white actresses hike up their dresses as they
      scurry for cover under the wagons, the men say words like
      "Gol' darn."

1926 Mose YellowHorse tosses his last professional pitch (with
      Omaha of the Western League) on May 1.

      Strangely enough, a "Yellowhorse" Morris shows up pitch-
      ing in the Negro Leagues. Morris enjoys his best season in
      1927 with the Detroit Stars, posting a mark of 14-8.[1]

1875 Thomas YellowHorse, who will become Mose's father, is
      five years old, and he is being made to walk from Nebraska

to Indian Territory (in Oklahoma). He will walk some four hundred miles in late summer across Nebraska, Kansas, and Oklahoma.

The Plains have a tendency to shimmer in August and September.

1898   Moses YellowHorse is born on January 28. *Nawa*, his parents say to him. And Clara YellowHorse, his mother, gives him a Christian name after a Hebrew revolutionary.

1916   Four days after YellowHorse's eighteenth birthday his mother, Clara Rickets YellowHorse, dies. Her father's name was *E-coos-stah-tus*. Her mother was known as *Stah-coo-de-wah*.

Clara was 52.

1921   It's April 21, the Pirates' home opener, and YellowHorse becomes the first rookie in team history (dating back to 1882) to win a home opener. He pitches 3 & 2/3 innings and gives up one run as the Pirates come from behind to win 8-7. In the team locker room after the game, all the boys slap him on the back. They will insist (later that night) that he celebrate by throwing back (his first) shots of whiskey.

1945   One night, for whatever reason, YellowHorse quits drinking. He will later say, "I've been very proud that I quit. Today I'm one of the happiest men in the world. I go here and there without fear and the people I meet and get to know have grown close to me."[2]

He drinks lots of soda after 1945.

1917   . . . is a busy year for the YellowHorses:

Mose attends Chilocco Indian School.

Meanwhile, Thomas sells his allotment lands to H. E. Miller.

And then, in the summer, Mose starts pitching for the Ponca City Oilers, a semipro team.

What's more, Thomas marries Bertha GoodFox (who is four years older than Mose) on August 28, and on December 22 she gives birth to a son, Lloyd YellowHorse, half-brother to Mose.

1919   There are records, too, showing that Mose was a war veteran. They say, "Called on the first day of the armistice and not assigned." And on another page titled "Remarks No. 2," it says that YellowHorse "Was only in the service three days."

1935   On March 28, in the *Dick Tracy* comic strip, an Indian character named "Chief Yellowpony" first appears. YellowHorse and Chester Gould grew up in Pawnee together, but "Yellowpony" wears braids and speaks broken English. He says things like "Yellowpony no see you in many moons."

1922   YellowHorse is traded by Pittsburgh to Sacramento of the Pacific Coast League, along with three other players and $7,500.00, for Earl Kunz.

Kunz's major league career totals: 1-2 with a 5.52 earned-run average in 21 games.

1918   Thomas YellowHorse dies.

When YellowHorse is with the Pirates, however, he makes numerous references to his father, some of which remain: "Yellow[H]orse predicted that if the Pirates won the pennant [in 1921] his dad would come to ... town and pitch a tent in centerfield."

Thomas YellowHorse is 48.

1958   He wore #50 as a Pittsburgh Pirate. And one of his major league gloves will be donated to the Baseball Hall of Fame and Museum. The caption in the display case reads:

"Glove worn by Moses 'Chief' Yellowhorse, Pittsburgh Pirates, 1921-22, Pitcher."

He has a fielding average of .920.

1924   In Salt Lake City. On three warm-up pitches, YellowHorse enters a game in the ninth inning with his team leading 18-15 and the bases loaded. He later said,

"I went in and I threw just nine pitches, striking out in order John Peters, Tony Lazzeri, and Duffy Lewis."[3]

Though YellowHorse calls it "the finest job of pitching I ever did," it badly injures his arm—to the point that he never again pitches as effectively.

1922   Detroit, during an exhibition game on September 26 versus the Tigers, YellowHorse beans Ty Cobb. Some believe that this is his finest job of pitching. One account of the incident states that YellowHorse gets Cobb in the leg; other accounts have it that he hit Cobb either in the throat, the head, or right between the eyes.

1971   YellowHorse is inducted into the Oklahoma Sports Hall of Fame.

1920   For the Arkansas Travelers, YellowHorse pitches to a 21-7 record, which helps the team to its first Southern Association Championship. They play Fort Worth (of the Texas League) in the first Dixie League Series, but lose four games to two—YellowHorse winning both games for the Travelers.

1947   YellowHorse works as a groundskeeper for the Ponca City,

Oklahoma, baseball team, a Class D minor league affiliate of the Brooklyn Dodgers.

And earlier in the spring:

Jackie Robinson breaks the "color line" with the Brooklyn Dodgers.

1964   YellowHorse dies on April 10.

1994   After more than ten attempts, the Pawnee Nation finally convinces the committee of the American Indian Athletic Hall of Fame that YellowHorse belongs.

He would have been ninety-six.

. . .

Notes

1   According to *The Biographical Encyclopedia of Baseball*, Harold "Yellowhorse" Morris pitched in the Negro Leagues from 1924 to 1936 with the Kansas City Monarchs, Detroit Stars, Chicago American Giants, and Monroe Monarchs.

2   Reprinted in Bob Lemke, "Pirates Pitcher Went 'Way of all Bad Injuns,'" *The Bleacher Bum: Sports Collectors Digest*, 3 Mar. 1994.

3   Reprinted in Bob Lemke, "Pirates Pitcher Went 'Way of all Bad Injuns,'" *The Bleacher Bum: Sports Collectors Digest*, 3 Mar. 1994.

Considering Contexts:
A Moment of Pawnee

PLACING MOSE YELLOWHORSE WITHIN HIS OWN COMMUNITY'S PAWNEE context is not an easy task, especially since the man and so many of his fellow tribal members, those who knew him, are no longer living. How much easier it would be if someone could ask YellowHorse: *How did your Pawnee way of life help you get along from one moment to the next, from one stage of life to the next?*

From various accounts and sources, however, it's nearly possible to establish the historical context and cultural milieu from which YellowHorse emerged. Given the tribe's structure and millennium-long history, their dealings with both Indian tribes and whites, their ceremonies and systems of belief, and their seasonal and daily routines a sketchy representation becomes much clearer.

For one, the Pawnees were historically divided into four bands: the *Skidi* (or Wolf Band), the *Kitkihahki* (or Little-Earth-Lodge Band, also known as the Republican Band), the *Chaui*, also spelled *Tsawi* (or Asking-for-Meat Band, also known as the Grand Pawnees), and the *Petahauirata*, also spelled *Pitahawirata* (or the Man-Going-Downstream Band, also known as the Tappage Band). Of these, YellowHorse belonged to the Skidi Band. According to tribal and nontribal accounts, the Skidi split off from the other three bands, though all four are said to have come from the South—whether the Southeast or Southwest is disputed. The Skidis, known as the northern band (the other three are referred to as southern bands), were the first to settle in present-day Nebraska. At different historical points along the way, the tribe lived in areas of present-day Texas, Oklahoma (pre-contact), Kansas, and finally Nebraska, and may have been the first Indians on the Great Plains. Like most communities, the Pawnees conducted trade, first with other Indian

tribes and later with whites. In 1541, the Pawnees even encountered Coronado while the Spanish colonist was in search of a
fictional "city of gold," one of the craftiest jokes (of self-preserva-
tion) ever devised by the Pueblos.

Though it is often easy to assume that the Pawnees carried out
various tasks as a single unit, tribal documents state that "Each
band went on separate hunts and often fought separate battles"
(www.pawneenation.org). Such battles were often waged against
the tribe's traditional enemies, including the Sioux, Cheyenne, Ara-
paho, Kiowa, Comanche, and Osage. By the mid-eighteenth
century, it is presumed that the other three bands joined the Skidis
in Nebraska—a result of declining trade opportunities with the
French and other Indian tribes. While each band lived in separate
villages, and even smaller clan villages, they all developed dome-
shaped earth lodges in which to live. During the spring and fall
seasons, when planting and harvesting crops, they built or refur-
bished lodges "with a diameter of twenty-five to sixty feet with a
long entrance to the east" that "housed extended families"
(www.pawneenation.org). While migrating during summer and
winter hunts, most lived in teepees. Each hunt was a large migra-
tory production, all supplies and family members packed for
months on the trail. Sometimes the hunting party stretched for
miles across the prairie—dogs, horses, and people all packed and
walking (usually south and west) in search of buffalo.

With the opening of the Louisiana Purchase in 1803, whites
began migrating west, and the tribe was typically friendly with
both settlers and government officials. The tribe's website states,
"Although the Pawnees never waged open war against the U.S. Government and were classified as a 'friendly nation,' extra privileges
were not gained" (www.pawneenation.org). In fact, not long after
the Purchase opened, the tribe was stricken with smallpox and
cholera, and their population, which had been close to 12,500, was
nearly wiped out, declining to some 2,800 by the end of the Civil
War. This decline, in combination with ongoing conflicts against
other tribes, most notably the Sioux, forced the Pawnees to cede

their lands unwillingly; as a result, the tribe signed treaties with the government in 1833, 1848, 1857, and 1872. Finally, in 1874 and 1875, they were removed to Indian Territory and settled in their present location.

YellowHorse's parents, Thomas and Clara, both children at the time of removal, made the trek from Nebraska to Oklahoma, probably during the summer of 1875, as the elderly and young were the last to leave. Though the Pawnees' journey was not nearly as long as other tribes', numerous people died along the way, and with the 1879 census count the tribe's population was at 1,440, a fifty-percent decline in less than fifteen years.

Once in Oklahoma, the routines of daily tribal life changed dramatically, not surprisingly. Schools were established (one boarding school and two day schools), including the Pawnee Industrial School, which became affectionately known as "Gravy U," and were attended by numerous Pawnee and non-Pawnee children. The government expected tribal members to live a stationary life, not just in the spring and fall, (as they had done for thousands of years) but year-round. That meant summer and winter hunts were no longer allowed, and since most of the buffalo herds had been hunted to near extinction, the tribe had little opportunity to conduct large expeditions. Though numerous families built earth lodges shortly after their arrival, the construction of such dwellings was usually discouraged (some structures were destroyed). Officials at the agency encouraged members to build wooden frame farmhouses and to learn agricultural or mechanical trades (for men) and home economic trades (for women). In short, the Pawnees, like every other Indian nation, were being forced by the federal government to assimilate. No other government policy exemplified this as did the Dawes Act (or General Allotment Act) of 1887. With this, each Indian allottee would receive 160 acres of land, United States citizenship (eventually), as well as $50 to build a house and for seed for two years; in addition, each family received two cows, a pair of ox or two mares, a set of harness, one plow, one wagon, one harrow, one hoe, one axe, and one pitchfork. Also, $3 million was deposited in the U. S. Treasury as a permanent fund for educational purposes.

Though much of the Pawnee way of life and culture was greatly threatened (even destroyed) as a result of the government's policies, many of the traditional ceremonies, rituals, and beliefs survived. As Muriel H. Wright notes, in a rather stilted manner, in *A Guide to the Indian Tribes of Oklahoma,*

> the Pawnee were notable for their tribal religion, rich in myth, symbolism, and poetic fancy, with elaborate rites and dramatic ceremonies connected with the cosmic forces and heavenly bodies. They believed that all these were created by the one deity, the all-powerful and all-present "Tirawa." Religious beliefs were highly integrated with most of the tribal institutions and practices—medicine, secret societies, war parties, buffalo hunting, construction of earth-covered lodges for dwellings, the planting and the growing of corn, marriage, games, feasts, and government. (203)

A bit archaic, Wright's passage nonetheless offers a general overview about the importance of astronomy and its religious implications in the Pawnee culture. According to another source, the Pawnee "were the star people of the Plains. . . . [T]hey developed more elaborate star ceremonies and rituals than any other tribe. The stars and constellations were a great influence on almost every aspect of their lives, and even their houses were laid out in patterns which duplicated the patterns of the constellations, including the position of their most important star gods" (hoa.aavso.org/spacetalk.htm).

Aside from the significance that astronomy played in their everyday lives, the Pawnees were also adept in the agricultural arts (both pre-contact and pre-removal), as some varieties of their seeds are still used today. Also, it is believed that modern-day powwows evolved out of a nineteenth-century Pawnee ceremony—the *Irushka,* meaning "they are inside the fire"—which was facilitated by their medicine society. Furthermore, "the Calumet Ceremony, which has come down in American common speech as the peace pipe, spread from the Pawnees" (Ballentine 272). It is also worth noting that the Pawnee Nation also takes great pride in the men who served as Pawnee Scouts, and who, at the government's behest, helped track down traditional Pawnee enemies during the mid-to-late nineteenth century. Given all this, it's safe to say that Pawnee culture and society, with all its belief systems, religious rituals and ceremonies, thrived. And still today, many practices remain.

A star-gazing and ceremonially active nation, the Pawnees developed many practices, whether ritualistic or practical, that came to be borrowed by other tribes across the Plains. In this way, they epitomize a number of philosophies and traditions that have become familiar to many.

It should be no surprise, then, to find that Mose YellowHorse was familiar with certain songs and ceremonies. He certainly knew about various rituals and traditions. Exactly how all this informed his life, his day-to-existence, is not totally clear. Suffice it to say, it can be determined with a degree of certainty that he embraced various aspects of his Pawnee heritage, as his later life demonstrates. From several interviews and tapes, it is obvious that YellowHorse became a respected individual in the Pawnee community, that he was a cultural caretaker, and for this to occur, he had to have been knowledgeable about and responsible with different kinds of information. He was, after all, born at a time when a good number of the older people were still active; as such, he no doubt learned about many of the old ways. Though the Pawnees were quick to adopt some aspects of Euroamerican culture, this was not done at the expense of memory. Millennium-old practices were not put aside and forgotten just because the community recognized a need to adapt and survive.

With this, the Pawnee culture, and many of their ceremonies and beliefs, remains intact today. Numerous songs, dances, games, and other traditional ways continue to be practiced. The language, which YellowHorse was fluent in, is taught all the time (and spoken) by members of all ages. Though the government tried with the Pawnees (as it did with every Indian nation) to subdue and rid the culture of its rituals and other practices, it did not succeed. Stories are still told, dances danced, songs sung, and ceremonies observed. This will be the case for a long time.

A Dancing Red Spine,
and Other Convergences

MOSE YELLOWHORSE PITCHED IN THIRTY-EIGHT MAJOR LEAGUE BASEBALL games—winning eight and losing four, with an earned run average of 3.93—for the Pittsburgh Pirates in 1921 and 1922, which hardly qualifies as a distinguished career. In fact, most of his appearances came as a relief pitcher at a time when relievers played much lesser roles than today. Usually washed-up starters at the ends of their careers, relievers were more like part-time pitchers, part-time coaches, and part-time pranksters who kept their teams' clubhouses lively. That YellowHorse pitched mostly out of the bull pen at the beginning of his career is a bit unusual, but as Pittsburgh manager George Gibson noted at the time, the team wanted to bring him along slowly.[1] Of the thirty-eight games in which YellowHorse pitched, he started nine and completed three. And despite the modesty of his major league career totals, YellowHorse initially showed great promise: at Chilocco Indian School in Oklahoma, near the Kansas border, he pitched to a 17-0 record in 1917; in 1920, with the Arkansas Travelers of the Southern Association, he won 21 and lost 7, while helping lead the team to its first League championship. YellowHorse's manager with the Travelers, Kid Elberfeld, who had played in the American League and batted against Walter Johnson, went so far as to assert that YellowHorse's fastball was as quick as Johnson's.[2] Elberfeld was not alone in his assertions; Pittsburgh catcher Wally Schmidt said that YellowHorse had "more stuff than any twirler he had ever handled."[3] In other words, YellowHorse's pitching abilities exceeded those of many other pitchers on the Pirate staff, including Babe Adams, Wilbur Cooper, and Johnny Morrison—all superb pitchers in their day, all twenty-game winners, one season or another. With a quick fastball, "a sweet curve too,"[4] and "an exceptional knowledge of baseball strategy,"[5] YellowHorse, it seems, should have accomplished much more during his major league career.

That his name is not as familiar as other Native American baseball players like Charles Bender, a Hall-of-Fame pitcher for the Philadelphia Athletics, John Meyers, even Louis Sockalexis, or Jim Thorpe, might be considered a disappointment. Yet the accolades given YellowHorse, especially after his death in 1964, make an impressive list: in 1994, he was inducted into the American Indian Athletic Hall of Fame; in Pawnee, where he was born and died, the tribe has recently dedicated a softball field in his honor; in 1974, the town also named a street after him.

In some ways, such a list is not surprising. Many major league players with brief careers become local celebrities, especially when they return to the towns where they grew up. Because they usually achieve a certain degree of amateur success within their hometowns and states, then professional success, such players are often inducted into local halls of fame, like the Oklahoma Sports Hall of Fame. While such players are usually fortunate to receive even one display of public affirmation, YellowHorse received several. That various cross-cultural institutions acknowledged YellowHorse's achievements suggests that his accomplishments touched a range of people—Pawnee tribal members, other Indians, as well as non-Indians. Though valuable records (such as box scores and old newspaper accounts) concerning YellowHorse's baseball career can be found in the Research Center at the Baseball Hall of Fame and Museum and in the archives of both *The Sporting News* and the Pittsburgh Pirates, the Pawnee Tribal elders who best knew him offer documentation through their stories and oral narratives and personal accounts that allow the fullest description of YellowHorse's character to emerge. Where newspaper accounts offer a kind of skeletal structure of YellowHorse's career and of his life after baseball, the stories told by the tribal elders serve as connective tissue, as the muscles and tendons that provide definition to YellowHorse's character.

Since YellowHorse did not have any children and did not leave any journals or other writings, the only way to know him is through numbers and stories: numbers in box scores and stories from the memories of Pawnee men and women who lived around him. And YellowHorse's life is worth examining because of the details, the specific narratives that merge between and through the many numbers. These details become entwined to create a life full of unusual cross-cultural intersections, convergences that involve Euroamerican and Native American politics and history, as well as American popular culture (Wild West shows, baseball, and *Dick Tracy*), and cultural preservation (Pawnee oral stories and tribally generated printed matter). The Mose YellowHorse who emerges out of such complicated entanglements is not easily reduced to American Indian (Pawnee) baseball player—that is just one of many starting points. In fact, YellowHorse is an orphan, a child stage performer, a World War I veteran, a hunter, a problem drinker (and later a nondrinker), an arena director, a groundskeeper, an Oklahoma state employee, a former Pittsburgh Pirate, Arkansas Traveler, Sacramento Solon, and a prankster. The many stories told by tribal elders touch on these matters with an urgency that is both serious and humorous. Their stories depict a YellowHorse who is both mythic and tragic, both a "down to earth" guy and a good storyteller.

To understand fully the significance of YellowHorse's accomplishments (from a Pawnee, or non-Pawnee point of view), it is necessary to understand the specific historical context of the moment during which he played his major league career. The 1920s, as they can be considered some seven or eight decades later, are generally identified (with a large dose of nostalgia) as a time of political and social extremes—the "Roaring 20s," as it has come to be known. At the beginning of the decade, with the end of World War I, the onset of Prohibition, the economy deep into delusional grandiosity, and the rise of the Jazz Age—all its frivolity and cheer —most Euroamericans felt good about the country's state of affairs. In 1921, when YellowHorse began his career with the Pirates, Babe Ruth hit 59 home runs (and 16 triples), Sacco and Vanzetti were found guilty of murder, Graham McNamee broadcast the first radio play-by-play of a baseball game at the Polo Grounds in New York, playwright Karel Capek coined the term robot in his play *RUR*, F. Scott Fitzgerald's *This Side of Paradise* caught the attention of young readers who imagined themselves as willing participants in his early novels, and speakeasies began to undermine the totalitarian goals of the Eighteenth Amendment. Given the unstable tenor of this period, Euroamericans tend to remember the early 1920s as a time of decadence and prosperity—flappers, the rise of Hollywood as one of the country's primary social shapers, the sleek lines of Art Deco, with a mind toward idolization of technology and machinery —as a self-congratulatory time when the country's understanding of its own well-being was overinflated. Of course, in more rural parts of the country, small communities that depended on agriculture as a means of survival did not experience such prosperous fortunes.

For Mose YellowHorse, the Euroamerican atmosphere of the early 1920s he entered was at once volatile and unusual. The Pawnee Nation, as it was situated both socially and politically in the early 1900s and through the late teens, had not shared in Euroamerica's prosperity, or false prosperity. In the span of fifty-four years from 1846 to 1900, the tribe's total population decreased by 95 percent, from an estimated 12,500 to 650. The explanations are familiar, yet still disturbing: disease and displacement—from both their traditional lands in Nebraska and their culture— account for most of the tribe's population decline. The Pawnees were, as Jefferson and Franklin had imagined a hundred years earlier with the eastern Indian tribes, a "vanishing race." Unfortunately, it is no surprise to find similar sentiments in the articles written by white sports writers of the 1920s—some 125 years later. One 1921 headline about YellowHorse reads, "LO, THE INDIAN REAPPEARS."[6] Such a statement, from a certain angle, seems to assert that Indians might have disappeared not only from baseball but from the North American continent. The headline writer suggests that it is surprising to find an Indian playing baseball. It could be also that the writer's making flippant use of a common phrase.

YellowHorse, however, was not immaculately conceived. According to Pawnee tribal enrollment documents, Thomas Yellow-Horse's father, *Ke-wah-koo-lah-lah-be-koo-chu*, died before allotment, sometime before 1887, and his mother is (un-)identified as "Unknown." As for Clara YellowHorse, her "Individual History Card," the form used by the Bureau of Indian Affairs (B.I.A.) agents to identify genealogy and allotment numbers, no longer exists, gone for whatever reason. How his parents met, courted, married, and the demeanor of their relationship remains a bit of a mystery. That they survived both the tribe's removal from Nebraska and the first five years in Indian Territory is somewhat surprising, since, as George Hyde notes, over 800 Pawnee died within those first years of displacement (365). As Hyde describes it, "Poverty, sickness, [and] deaths in every family ... had thoroughly demoralized the tribe" (341). That "nearly all the deaths were due to the weakening effects of lack of food, clothing, and proper shelter" (344) is a common refrain. The Pawnees, like so many tribes removed from their homes and land, had little influence when appealing to the U.S. government for help, especially when the government's policies displayed both deliberate indifference and calculated hostility. The government had no interest in helping people it expected to disappear. (Examples of U.S. policy regarding the so-called "Indian Problem" are many and well-documented.[7])

By the time, then, that YellowHorse reached his teens, the situation in Pawnee was bleak. He attended the agency boarding school on Pawnee tribal grounds, and whether or not he went through tribulations similar to those discussed by numerous Native authors[8] is not known, though it is probable that the agency's teachers (who were employed by the government) treated Indian kids in Pawnee the same as other teachers in other tribal communities, that is, with the stern stick of acculturation. In all likelihood, YellowHorse's experience was probably not as difficult as it was for Indian children in other schools across the country. As

Douglas Parks notes in his Introduction to George Dorsey's *The Pawnee Mythology*, "By 1890 most of the Skiris [or Skidis] . . . were living in houses on their own farms," as was the case with the YellowHorses. Most Skidis were "dressing like contemporary whites, and speaking English in daily life. Some children were attending the local Pawnee Industrial Boarding School, at which they received a minimal education" (xiii). Forty years earlier, in his *The Pawnee Indians*, George Hyde wrote, "The Skidis were progressive; [which meant that] two-thirds of them spoke English, dressed like whites, furnished their houses like whites, had buggies, mowing machines, and reapers" (346). In Hyde's view, progressivism equaled assimilation and was viewed in positive terms (not in terms of displacement) as the "advancement" of a "savage people" to "civilized" or Euroamerican "ways." To be progressive, that is reform-minded, meant putting aside of some the Skidi Pawnees' cultural traditions. What was really at stake, of course, was survival. Mariah Gover, a Skidi Pawnee/Tohona O'odham, remembers that her great-grandfather, who was born about the same time as YellowHorse, valued education a great deal, "as a way for the Skidis to get ahead."[9] Just because the Skidi band believed (and still believe) in the Euroamerican education system as a means to survive first, then prosper later, did not mean that they totally dismissed their cultural traditions. Though Mose YellowHorse was not one to dance or sing, he certainly enjoyed watching others participate in keeping such traditions alive. And by the time YellowHorse advanced to the major leagues in 1921, he had been off Pawnee grounds enough and had presumably grown up in an environment that valued certain aspects of Euroamerican education, so that the white culture into which he entered was not totally foreign—perhaps just a bit strange, but still untrustworthy. Though he had survived what must have been a trying childhood, YellowHorse is described by many tribal members' stories as having a pastoral, even bucolic, existence: a boy on his father's farm doing chores, yet having the time to go hunting near Black Bear Creek, also on his father's farm, and developing a strong arm by throwing rocks at small animals, such as rabbits, squirrels, snakes, crows, etc.

The historical context, then, of YellowHorse's experiences up to 1921 is complex. The white culture into which he entered was full of economic confidence, euphoric about the recent conclusion of the war, and rebellious against Prohibition. The Skidi Pawnee culture from which he emerged, while devastated because of displacement and disease, sought survival through education—a system through which YellowHorse endured and finally succeeded, concluding his final year at Chilocco Indian School with a diploma. With baseball stops in Des Moines and Little Rock before Pittsburgh, YellowHorse, so it seems, might have been prepared for the rigors of big league life, for traveling three months out of a six-month season, for living out of a suitcase, for keeping to strict curfews, and "keeping in shape." As both the elders' stories and newspaper accounts show, that would not be the case.

The situation in which YellowHorse found himself, as a Pawnee and as a baseball player in a large, industrial, Eastern city, was at once foreign, exhilarating, and frightening. In drawing an accurate conclusion about YellowHorse's circumstances in 1921, it must be remembered that YellowHorse was a twenty-three-year-old orphan, whose mother and father had passed away by the time he was twenty. He was culturally displaced and isolated in Pittsburgh, since no Pawnees accompanied him, and he was suddenly financially secure as a ballplayer, earning well above the national income average.[10] Given these factors, it is not too difficult to imagine that he might have been susceptible to veteran players who had already adjusted to the day-to-day demands of living as major leaguers.

The veteran player YellowHorse gravitated to was Walter "Rabbit" Maranville, a shortstop acquired in a trade with the Boston Braves two months before the beginning of the 1921 season. Maranville, who would be posthumously elected to the Hall of Fame in 1954 (he died January 5, 1954), was a starting member of the 1914 "Miracle Braves," which moved from last place on July 4

to first place by the end of that season to capture the National
League pennant, and then defeated the Philadelphia Athletics 4
games to 0 in the World Series. Though Maranville was as well
known for his off-the-field antics as for his base stealing and flashy
glove work at short, his World Series experience made him a valuable addition to Pittsburgh roster. Team owner Barney Dreyfuss felt
the benefits of Maranville's experiences outweighed the shortstop's reputation as a prankster and drinker. The fact that
Maranville's acquisition coincided with YellowHorse's joining the
Pirates made for a combustive entanglement, one that would later
foster many good stories but that at the time allowed the two men
to form a friendship based as much on mutual admiration as on
their need to feel secure in unfamiliar surroundings. They were
both high-spirited ballplayers who fed off each other's energy.
Sometimes that energy manifested itself in outrageous competi-
tions; sometimes they played practical jokes on other players
(either the Pirates, or opposing teams); sometimes they drank too
much; sometimes they got into fights. Regardless of the situation,
both YellowHorse and Maranville provoked in each other a mis-
chievous tendency. It is likely, given their age difference[11] and the
difference in their major league experience,[12] that Maranville was
the instigator in a number of pranks, at least initially. Maranville,
older and more seasoned, perhaps saw in YellowHorse a like-
minded partner—someone young, strong, funny, and smart
enough to act impulsively in tandem with him. Perhaps YellowHorse saw in Maranville a fun-loving and quick-thinking wit
who seemed to take a genuine interest in his career and success.

Regardless of the reasons why they were first drawn to one
another, the two men enjoyed spending time together, to the point
that they became roommates on the road. Even when the team was
in Pittsburgh, they often had dinner together—going out after
games to eat and carouse around town. Usually, they ended up at a
speakeasy. Though Pittsburgh was no New York or Chicago, the
amount of raucous behavior not as great, the atmosphere that pre-
cipitated such behavior existed. In *Ardent Spirits*, John Kobler states

that eight Pittsburgh-area breweries during Prohibition "produced 10,000 gallons of ale and beer a day," so that "Pittsburgh ale lovers prided themselves on the quality of the ... brands available locally and cheerfully paid 75 cents to $1 a bottle" (235, 234). Certainly YellowHorse and Maranville consumed their share of that daily production. And many stories mention the enjoyment they derived from drinking together and clowning around at all times of the day.

In several stories that involve both YellowHorse and Maranville, writers Fred Lieb,[13] Pat Harmon,[14] who wrote for the *Cincinnati Post & Times-Star*, Mike Werries,[15] a sports writer in Pittsburgh, and Bob Lemke,[16] a writer for *Sports Collectors Digest*, each offer differing accounts of an outrageous contest between YellowHorse and Maranville in July of 1922. Each writer describes a situation in which the two players, while on the road to play either New York or Boston,[17] decided to hold a contest to see which of one them could catch the most pigeons bare-handed from a sixteenth-story ledge. As the story goes, they lured the birds with popcorn. Lieb suggests that "'Rab' and the Chief [sic] had eaten, then done the round of near-by 'speaks,' [and] got their fill of needled beer" before pulling their stunt (196). To intensify matters, once they caught the birds, they flung them into their two separate closets and then fell asleep. They did so knowing full well that their new manager, "Deacon" Bill McKechnie[18] (who decided to room with his two rowdiest players in order to settle them down), would arrive before the team curfew and be surprised to find them already sleeping. YellowHorse and Maranville also knew that he would eventually put his clothes away in one of the closets. When McKechnie finally did open one of the closets, the trapped pigeons flew into his face. Exactly how he reacted to a flock of trapped pigeons coming at him and then responded to YellowHorse and Maranville isn't known, but all four writers state that McKechnie no longer roomed with the players following this incident. Shortly after, the Pirates began a sustained winning streak that allowed them to enter the National League's upper division and to compete for the pennant. As for who won the contest, it seems Maranville caught more pigeons than YellowHorse (8 to 5) but was good enough to "share his 80-proof winnings" with Mose anyway.

Another story, one which involves only YellowHorse, was told by tribal elder Earl Chapman and centers on YellowHorse's drinking during the Pirates' 1922 games—not while he was sitting out in the bull pen, but while he was on the field participating in a game. According to Chapman, "the groundskeepers in Pittsburgh would supply Mose with shots of whiskey when he was pitching." Apparently Mose would make some kind of gesture, perhaps having to do with the pitcher's mound needing more dirt here or there (in order for him to have the right footing to complete his pitching delivery), and the groundskeepers would come out to the mound and "put shots of whiskey all around the mound. And then he would sneak shots without anybody noticing. Nobody ever saw him do it. He never got caught."[19] What's intriguing about this story is that, on one level, it disregards probability. What is most important is the fact that YellowHorse gets away with such behavior. He performs a "taboo" act, especially in 1922, and he does so in front of fans, teammates, and opponents. Nobody, aside from his groundskeeping cohorts, realizes he is even doing something considered wrong. He never gets caught. He bucks the system and avoids any reproach. To make sense of such a story, it is important to remember, as Paula Gunn Allen (Laguna Pueblo) notes, that "within the tribal world of the contemporary or traditional American Indian, many statements that stem from the 'imagination' are taken to be true" (ix). In other words, the imagination is as viable a source of explanation of the past as is historical fact, in the Western sense. When Earl Chapman recounted this story, he offered me an account as trustworthy as a written story or a box score in the *New York Times*. As with other elders' YellowHorse stories, the hero of Earl Chapman's narrative becomes one in a whole tapestry of tales that establishes a mythic quality for many of YellowHorse's actions. He was capable of throwing back whiskey shots without anyone noticing. He could cajole the groundskeepers into doing him favors. He could fool people.

That 1922 season was the last in Pittsburgh for YellowHorse. Two months after the Pirates' disappointing campaign ended, he was traded to Sacramento of the Pacific Association.[20] Highlights from his two years in Pittsburgh include a victory versus Cincinnati in the Pirates' home opener on April 21, 1921. He also recorded victories against the Cubs, Philadelphia, Cincinnati (again), and Brooklyn in his first season. Unfortunately for YellowHorse, his rookie season came to an end in early July when he suffered an injury while pitching against St. Louis. The injury was serious enough to warrant surgery, which in those days meant he had no chance of returning to the pitching lineup. Since Pittsburgh finished second in the National League pennant chase in '21, YellowHorse also received an $839.97 World Series share—not a bad bonus for a solid rookie year. The most notable highlight of YellowHorse's 1922 season came when he beaned Ty Cobb in a late-season exhibition game against the Detroit Tigers. Though the fans in Detroit were irate about the incident, YellowHorse's Pirate teammates rallied around him when a bench-clearing brawl ensued.

In 1923, he posted a 22-13 record for Sacramento, completed 19 games, and continued to impress people with a 3.68 earned-run average. Such numbers were certainly strong enough to interest major league teams, but no takers called. In all likelihood, the reputation YellowHorse established in Pittsburgh as a rowdy player was responsible. Such players—and there were many—were considered too big a risk to take on. Though many teams could have used YellowHorse's services, one call to the Pirates probably ended their interest. Finally, in 1924, YellowHorse suffered a debilitating arm injury at the beginning of Sacramento's season, an injury from which he never recovered. Later, that same season, YellowHorse was traded to Fort Worth. After several ineffective appearances, however, Fort Worth sent him back to Sacramento. He then started the 1925 season with Mobile, of the Southern Association, but was returned to Sacramento. In January 1926, Sacramento sold him to Omaha. His final game for Omaha came on May 1, against Tulsa, and he lasted only two and one-third innings. He gave up five runs, on six hits, and was charged with the loss. With this appearance, YellowHorse's professional baseball career ended.

By most accounts, he then returned to Pawnee, where he took on odd jobs, lived with different friends, and spent a good deal of time drinking. It seems that YellowHorse, like so many professional athletes, had a difficult time adjusting to life after baseball. The Pawnee elders with whom I spoke did not share many stories from this period of YellowHorse's life. Whether this is because there's not much to tell about a person's drinking behavior or because the stories aren't for sharing is not clear. It is likely that many Pawnees were disappointed in what they perceived as YellowHorse's failure to achieve his athletic potential. The stories that still circulate about this period in his life are fairly grim. For instance, I listened to two women talk about YellowHorse's hitting his supposed wife, Beatrice Epple, so hard in the throat that she couldn't talk for a month. Though injured, she still had enough gumption to order YellowHorse to leave the house, for good. The two women who told me this story went on for some time in hushed tones, shaking their heads, disturbed still over the story they had heard others tell them.

From 1927 until 1945, then, YellowHorse's worked at odd jobs, earning enough money to drink and to eat. Time and again while I listened to accounts of these years, an elder would shake his or her head after mentioning YellowHorse's drinking problem. "He drank too much," was a common refrain. Yet no one spent much time elaborating on the point. Throwing around images of an intoxicated YellowHorse would do nothing but perpetuate the stereotype of the drunken Indian.

The fact is, YellowHorse quit drinking cold turkey in 1945. Even though Pawnee elders do not tell many stories from this period in YellowHorse's life, it is obvious that they, too, are proud of YellowHorse for overcoming his drinking problem. Norman Rice said he never remembered seeing YellowHorse drink, which makes sense, considering that Rice was born in the mid-30s.[21] Anna Mulder, a longtime friend of YellowHorse, would not discuss the matter. Instead, she focused on other narratives, like the fact that he often went to her house and chopped wood, mowed the yard, or fixed broken appliances. Other elders simply refused to discuss this period in his life altogether.

The one event from this period about which everyone is familiar occurred in 1935, when a character based on YellowHorse appeared in the *Dick Tracy* comic strip. Since *Tracy* creator Chester Gould was born and grew up in Pawnee, it came as no surprise to the locals that Gould would include a YellowHorse-based character in the strip. Gould had always included aspects of his hometown in the cartoon, and local merchants often recognized their storefronts in Gould's drawings. However, the Yellowpony character bears little resemblance to YellowHorse, except for his physical build. Gould, who grew up around Indians and maintained close friendships with many tribal members, chose to represent a Yellowpony wearing braids and beadwork and talking with a thick accent. For example, when Yellowpony departs from the strip, he says to Tracy, "Ugh! Big bad gunmen end up helpless bunch of bones. Crime bad medicine! Always lead to same place, long dark night underground! Ugh!"[22] Of course, YellowHorse did not speak with a "Carlisle English" accent. But Gould constructed a Yellowpony character who looked and talked as Euroamericans of the 1930s expected a "real Indian" to look and talk. Aside from these obvious stereotypic characteristics, Yellowpony was cast a hero who helped Tracy capture Boris and Zora Arson, two escaped convicts. Though he was introduced as a naive character (he fell for one of Boris Arson's cons at some point in the past), Yellowpony developed into an ardent crime fighter—shooting villains and helping Tracy plot the capture of various criminals.

Since YellowHorse and Gould were so close in age, it's no surprise to find that they were close friends. According to Gladys Kitchen, a volunteer at the Pawnee County Historical Society, the two men got along quite well, to the point that "Mose'd sometimes visit Chester in Woodstock, Illinois." Tribal member Becky Eppler

stated that Mose "thought [the appearance of Yellowpony] was
funny" and that "it wasn't a big deal." From both views, it seems
safe to assume that YellowHorse probably wasn't disappointed
with Gould's development of a character who did not really bear
any resemblance to himself. To see the appearance of a character
based on his likeness must have been exciting on one level.
Because so many elders speak proudly of the Yellowpony episodes,
it is likely that YellowHorse, too, got some kind of kick out of them.
After all, if YellowHorse had been disappointed with the character,
he could have shared his feelings with others, including Chester
Gould. With a span of over sixty years after the appearance of Yellowpony, elders continue to share the story enthusiastically, out of
respect for YellowHorse.

For more than a decade, YellowHorse continued to drift from
odd job to odd job, from one person's home to another. Following
his return to Pawnee in 1926, YellowHorse, according to many of
the stories, refined his own brand of aimlessness to an art form.
Though he was well liked, his shenanigans wore thin with many
people. Nineteen years of licking the clichéd wound of "unfulfilled
potential" must have made YellowHorse weary, too. Unable to
shake the feeling, even with excursions to Tulsa, a powwow, or dinner at someone's house, YellowHorse, like so many, must have
gotten—as the saying goes—sick and tired of being sick and tired.
Then in 1945, after more than twenty years of drinking, he decided
to quit. If YellowHorse became a "friend of Bill W." and attended
A.A. meetings, no one has said. The fact is, when speaking of YellowHorse's drinking, people in Pawnee employ particularly
extreme tones, depending on the period they are discussing. For
example, elder Pawnees, when talking about YellowHorse's drinking within the context of his playing days, tend to speak playfully.
They make light of it and smile about his antics with Rabbit
Maranville. YellowHorse was, after all, a small-town kid spending
every night in a big city, Pittsburgh or somewhere on the road, and
drinking under such circumstances is viewed as nothing more
than a young man's curiosity. Nonetheless, most elders identify

drinking as the primary reason for the brevity of YellowHorse's promising major league career. When the conversation turns to "what could have been," most tribal members usually shake their heads, signifying some slight disappointment that YellowHorse failed to become the next Bender or Walter Johnson.

Once Yellowhorse quit drinking, the momentum of his life changed, too. He found steady work, first with the Ponca City farm team, then with the Oklahoma State Highway Department. He continued, however, to move from household to household, a pattern that seemed to suit him just fine. He also discovered that people in those different regions of the country where he had played remembered his accomplishments fondly. He found that people were ready, even willing, to celebrate what he had achieved during his playing days—no matter how modest his major league career totals. He was startled to realize that the fans and team administrators in Sacramento continued to appreciate his tenure with the Solons. When "Mose YellowHorse Night" was celebrated in Sacramento, when the Pittsburgh Pirates invited YellowHorse to attend a World Series game, and when he traveled to Little Rock, fans at each stop displayed enough gratitude to please anyone. Bill Conlin, a retired sports editor at the *Sacramento Bee*, stated that YellowHorse surprised everyone when, on his visit in 1958, he told them that he didn't drink anymore.[23] As Conlin put it, "Sam Gordon [the team's owner] ordered enough whiskey to intoxicate an army. When YellowHorse told him that he didn't drink anymore, Sam, with a straight face, asked him what his favorite soda was and ordered two cases of it. In exchange, YellowHorse gave Sam a full traditional Indian headdress." It seems that variations of this routine also occurred in Pittsburgh and Little Rock.

From 1945 until his death in 1964, YellowHorse not only received tributes from various ball clubs, but he also got involved with organized baseball again. He became a groundskeeper for the Ponca City ball club (a class D Brooklyn Dodger affiliate) in 1947. And in 1950, he managed and coached "an all-Indian baseball team consisting mostly of teenage boys, all full-blood,"[24] which he took across Oklahoma and Arkansas, playing in semipro and exhibition games. In addition to these activities, he also umpired and tried to establish Little Leagues in Pawnee and other parts of the state. He filled his time, too, with hunting and fishing. As numerous Pawnee elders noted, YellowHorse loved to hunt and fish and sometimes preferred a rod and reel to a mitt and ball. In fact, as YellowHorse became more involved with baseball, he became more involved with the tribe, too. When he served for years as arena director for the Pawnee Homecoming celebration, he was as much an attraction as some of the dancers and singers. Time and again elders told me that some people came just to see him. Though he might not know everyone in attendance, YellowHorse was always willing to share a story, whether with an Indian or non-Indian. The fact is, YellowHorse, more than any elder or sports writer, shared stories and details of his life with many people. He often initiated, even promoted, certain aspects of his life. He became proud of what he had accomplished without letting it define his whole character. YellowHorse remained thankful for his opportunities and achievements, but he no longer pined over what could have been. As he matured, he took in the various tributes and did not become big headed. As Pawnee tribal member Norman Rice said, "Mose always remained a nice guy. Not overly proud of what he did."[25]

By the time YellowHorse died on April 10, 1964, many people in the tribe were aware of certain stories, of certain facts. In the decades since his death, these stories and facts represent a body of Pawnee narratives that describe YellowHorse as a lauded figure—whether the stories are positive or more critical. For instance, a number of accounts relay how YellowHorse ruined his arm. Numerous stories about his hunting abilities continue to circulate. In this way, tribal members commemorate YellowHorse's life with tributes that are informative. One of the most visible tributes is YellowHorse's headstone in the North Indian Cemetery in Pawnee. It was bought by Anna Mulder shortly after YellowHorse's death. Another visible tribute to YellowHorse was recently erected when the tribe named and dedicated a softball field in his honor.

Though he left no children and no writings, the life of Mose YellowHorse continues to be discussed in Pawnee, Oklahoma. It is probable that in Pittsburgh, Little Rock, Sacramento, and a few other places, stories of YellowHorse's baseball career continue to inform local baseball history. As Andy High, a former St. Louis player who faced YellowHorse in the National League, told *The Sporting News* in 1947, "I'll never forget what it meant to face that Indian with a bat in your hand" (Kaff 42). Such words suggest the uneasiness that batters had when trying to hit against YellowHorse. Such a context suggests larger issues, ones which reach back—and forward as well—to moments of Indian and white relations that are charged with historical tension. Not only is the pitcher/batter confrontation immediate, it also becomes a powerful metaphor. The figurative richness of Mose YellowHorse throwing a baseball toward the bodies of Ty Cobb, or Andy High, or Babe Ruth is heightened when such larger contexts come into play. The fact is, a baseball thrown over ninety miles per hour can be a weapon in the same way a bat can be a weapon. And a Pawnee man with some history on his mind might have an occasion to let a pitch or two get away. Though YellowHorse certainly focused on his goal of recording outs, he may have, from time to time, considered the mocking war whoops yelled by opposing players and fans, the stories his parents told him about relocation, and the dancing red spine of the baseball as it twirled from his hand.

.   .   .

Notes

1   Joe Vila, "Chief YellowHorse Is Indian Pitcher," *The Sporting News* 1921, writes, "Gibson, it is believed, will gradually ease him into a regular berth by sending him to the box as a relief sharpshooter."

2   According to Bill Conlin, retired sports writer for the *Sacramento Bee*, "When he pitched . . . there were those who said he threw as fast as Walter Johnson whose fastball then was the greatest in baseball." The quotation is reprinted in an article in the *Pawnee Chief*, 26 Aug. 1992.

3   Reprinted in Bob Lemke, "Pirates Pitcher Went 'Way of all Bad Injuns,'" *The Bleacher Bum: Sports Collectors Digest*, 3 Mar. 1994.

4   Reprinted in Lemke, from *The Sporting News*'s 1920 spring training report, in which the author states "The Indian has a sweet curve."

5   Vila, "Chief Yellow Horse Is Indian Pitcher."

6   The writer of the article is unidentified, but by studying the photocopied story from the Research Department of the Baseball Hall of Fame and Museum, the article appears to have been published in a Pittsburgh newspaper.

7   From Chief Joseph to Vine Deloria, Jr., from William Apess to George Copway.

8   Authors including Simon Ortiz, Revard, Silko, Vizenor, and many others consider such issues in their work.

9   Mariah Gover, Interview, 3 Mar. 1998.

10 The average income per U.S. household in 1920 was less than $900 per year.

11 YellowHorse was twenty-three at the time, while Maranville was twenty-nine.

12 While 1921 marked YellowHorse's first year in the majors, it was Maranville's tenth.

13 From Frederick J. Lieb's *The Pittsburgh Pirates*, which was published in 1948.

14 *Cincinnati Post & Times-Star*, "Chief Yellowhorse and the Rabbit," 24 Apr. 1964. Harmon opens his article by stating, "What this country needs is some more ballplayers like Moses Yellowhorse and his roommate, the Rabbit."

15 Mike Werries, "Yellowhorse: Indian with a Funny Bone," *Steel City Sports* 6 July 1973.

16 "Pirates Pitcher Went 'Way of all Bad Injuns,'" *The Bleacher Bum: Sports Collectors Digest*, 3 Mar. 1994.

17 Lieb reports that the incident took place in New York; Harmon states that the "contest" occurred during the team's "first night on the road"; Werries states "One report says it was in New York, another Boston;" and Lemke asserts "the team was in Boston."

18 George Gibson resigned his duties as Pirates manager on June 30, 1922, at which time team owner Barney Dreyfuss named McKechnie the new manager.

19 Interview, 16 June 1992.

20 In December, YellowHorse, along with three other players, was traded to Sacramento of the Pacific Association for Earl Kunz.

21 Norman Rice was born in 1936.

22 *Dick Tracy*, 22 May 1935.

23 Interview, 17 Sept. 1992.

24 *Arkansas Gazette* 17 May 1950.

25 Interview, 20 June 1992.

Some Beginnings

Cartoon of Mose YellowHorse, Arkansas Gazette, 1950

Of All Things Winter

On a January morning, you can't see the snow barely falling, or a
    wind pushing it
to a cabin's door. It's enough to catch the sound of a woman's voice
    from inside,
where she twists on a bed built in Tulsa, Oklahoma, where she
    pushes against the body
that's trying to fight out of her.

She glistens like a January moon as her hands press cosmologies
    into crisp bed sheets.
It's January 28, 1898. And the body trying to merge into its own
    breath, its own voice,
will soon feel snowflakes melting on its live tongue. But first
    there'll be moments of screaming.
There will be flights of imagination and prayers spoken in Pawnee.

There will be flashbacks to 1875, to moments when a young girl
    walked from Nebraska
to Indian Territory. And the images will go something like: the
    bones of children's fingers,
the bodies of cholera-filled Pawnee, and shallow graves undone by
    the shoveling feet
of scavenging birds.

And there will be other women standing around the bed. They'll
    wipe the woman's birth sweat
from her mouth and tell stories about their own children. The
    room will fill with aromas
and discussions of possible names. And their hands will be busy
    with wet cloths,
and one of them will crowd her palms beneath the body that shapes

itself one inch at a time into its own shoulders, hips, and feet. Steam
    will wind off the legs
and twirl off his tightly fisted hands, and his mother will say
    "Moses," and the other women
will say "YellowHorse." They'll laugh at the moment his father
    enters the room with eyes
as bright as suns.

When it's over, there's always food on the other side of a ceremony,
    always stories
about how the child'll grow, the possibilities, hopes that this one
    boy might somehow dazzle
the future. And there's little silence as the cabin door rattles.

Form 5-153, Family history of Thomas YellowHorse

How to Read a Population Table*

"These figures on Pawnee population are the best available."
  —George Hyde, *The Pawnee Indians*

YEAR	POP.	
1836	12,500	Official report.
1836	10,000	Missionary report.
1840	6,244	Missionary report. First actual count.
1846	12,500	Agent's report.
1847	8,400	Missionary estimate. Number of warriors in 1848.
1850	5,000	Agent's report: "4,000 to 5,000." 1,234 died of cholera in '49.
1860	4,000	Nebraska settlers' estimate.
1865	2,800	Number on annuity roll.
1870	3,000	George Bird Grinnell. Estimate.
1875	2,276	First census of tribe in Ind. Ter. Male, 866; female, 1,160.
1879	1,440	800 deaths in first five years in Ind. Ter.
1886	998	Births, 28; deaths, 77.
1890	804	Male, 380; female, 424; school children, 124.
1900	650	[blank]
1905	646	[blank]
1910	653	[blank]
1940	1,017	Males, 516; females, 501.

---

* George E. Hyde. *The Pawnee Indians*. Norman: U of Oklahoma P, 1974.

Please note: "The steady and dreadful loss in population from [1836] to 1905" (Hyde 364);

Notice, too: All figures are taken by: Tribal agents
                                             Missionaries
                                             Nebraska settlers
                                             George Bird Grinnell
                                           Census takers, but
                                             No Pawnees;

So that: Time x (Interaction with whites) + (Removal to Indian Territory) = 94.832 percent population decrease by 1905;

Consider, too: the YellowHorses make up .46 percent of the tribe's population in 1905, but by 1920, with a population count of 731, they make up less than .0027 percent;

Though both of Mose YellowHorse's parents died before 1920, on December 22, 1917 (after Clara had died on February 1, 1916 and Thomas remarried to Bertha Good Fox on August 28, 1917), Lloyd YellowHorse was born;

And suppose, also: as ethnohistorian Henry Dobyns suggests, total Indian populations (precontact) exceeded 112 million people, but by 1492 (after interaction with traders and other explorers) the population dropped to 18 million, and by 1900 it stood at some 350,000;

And remember that: the Pawnees had no need to count themselves, as they knew where each village encamped;

Then: after 1875, they had no need to count themselves, as they could see tribal members from their new front porch views.

. . .

Between lines
from one year
to the next
the numbers
dwindle like
late autumn sun-
light but they
don't present
any depth of
imagery none
of the ashes
from infection-
filled blankets
that were burned
along the way
between 1874
and 1875.

Maybe it's enough
to know that the
amounts of annuity
checks are eleven
bucks per year
for every enrolled
member as the 21st
century opens its
eyes and maybe
it's just enough to
know it's been that
way for decades
that the increasing
numbers of babies
mean more to aunts
& uncles than U.S.-
issued checks.

. . .

"In order to obtain the clearest reading of a 'Population Table' one must possess an ability to reckon the larger narratives inherent in both population increases and decreases.... Often times more advanced countries which have developed industries and the like decrease in numbers for the very fact that certain variables such as an increase in stress and responsibilities serve as barriers to intimacy. On the other hand those nations now called 'Third World' often increase in population due to tight living spaces.... In other instances some populations decrease because of trends related to an inability to adapt to various environments. In these cases the reader must gain a comprehensive understanding of historical context as it influences both the decreasing population and possible increasing populations."

—*Reading Civilizations and Societies Nearing the End of the Century,* 1974

Wild West Shows & Other Histories

"At the age of three he was with Pawnee Bill's wild west circus." *
—Norman E. Brown, on YellowHorse, in 1921

There's magic in the sentimental smack
of a boy's feet pattering on smooth ground,
in the pull of his arms and hands moving
him to a full sprint. There's magic, too,
in a barker's call, "Come one! Come all!"
and how it attracts thousands eager to part
with their skinny nickels. In 1901, that's
the only way to explain it, how they
scramble for peeks into italicized versions
of an American past. Boys in New York,
Boston, and Philadelphia are gawking at
the wonder of an arrow's spin snapping
into a man's body, and how minutes later
he'll rise again to wave at the crowd. 1901,
and Mose YellowHorse's job title reads
something like *savage Indian boy.* He's to
"run and scream" and to "keep his bow
and arrow ready for projection." He's
told this in English and Pawnee and nods
at both. But his eyes might be stretching
to the line of camels, to the waving ears
of African elephants. There's too much
to see—the Italian sword swallower
and Lady Weaver's blonde beard. During
the show's *Indian Attack,* he aims at white
actresses who hike up their dresses and
scurry for cover under authentic 1853 wagons.

---

* Pawnee Bill, whose real name was Major Gordon W. Lillie, owned and coordi-
nated his wild west show for a couple of decades and employed hundreds of
Indians from all over the continent.

Every night he hears stories and sleeps
between Pawnee men who've warned him
of old enemies: the Sioux, Cheyenne, Osage.
When he wakes in the mornings, he has no
idea how to measure three months. No way
of knowing when he'll return home to Black
Bear Creek. He doesn't know about money
zipping across the country to his waiting
parents, or the weight of hailstones bending
160 acres of wheat crops. He has no way
of knowing the extraordinary strength of his
fingers, that bowstrings might be a precursor
to the red seams of a baseball. When he hears
applause it might be like rattles of ancestral
music, sounds so clear in the distance they
will be hurled ninety-five miles per hour
into the future.

The Way Mose YellowHorse Learned how to Throw
along Black Bear Creek in Pawnee, Oklahoma Before
He Discovered the Meaning of a Fastball or Whistling
—after Albin LeadingFox, Pawnee elder and relative of Mose YellowHorse

Some mornings
there's a hint of myth in the air,
the way
horizons become
shapely spines,
the way
blowing maple limbs
turn their curved leaves
into faces, like
the exact profiles of crows
in flight. And farmyards
are the cartography
of childhood
in Indian Territory
in nineteen-hundred-and-six.
A boy
who is eight years old
will quietly cross
his dad's (allotted) land with his hands full
of round stones: he
has heard enough stories
to imagine himself into a hunter,
enough of the old
that's-the-way-it-went
to know how to track
a rabbit, squirrel, or snake.
And he
moves slowly

through the woods
with some kind of warrior
image twirling around his mind.
He will
return home
with an evening meal
of two rabbits & a crow
and tell his parents just how
he did it:
That bird
was a hundred feet away
sitting on a fence post,
and his parents
will say
Good,
now wash the dishes.
And he
learns how to whistle
from listening to rocks
fly out of his hand.

Thomas YellowHorse's house near Black Bear Creek in Pawnee, Oklahoma, ca. 1910

Something Pastoral (in 1917)

Baseball, a dancing red spine
eighty-seven miles per hour
divides the atmosphere in two.

This is Chilocco Indian School
on a sloping spring day, and horses
grazing out beyond the fences.

It's a kid named YellowHorse
and a fastball 60 feet, 6 inches
and other distances from home.

His pitches mystify three batters
per inning. One at a time
they walk away from home

plate shaking their heads, because
he's on his way to a perfect 17
and o season. The locals around

school call him *The Pulverizing*
Pawnee, and they say there's magic
in his right arm. It's an afternoon

of the Chilocco nine versus Henry
Kendall College and the sky four
shades of blue. YellowHorse tosses

one fastball after another, and his
teammates grow bored with strikes
one-two-and-three. They don't

know that his mind is fixed
on the sounds of his mother's stories,
her voice echoing as he follows

through on his fourteenth strike-
out of the game. Her voice says
something like *Your names come*

from two different worlds, as he
shakes off one curveball after
another. That's how performing

goes, the mind wanders during
the deepest states of concentration.
He might begin to think about

the slapping water of Black Bear
Creek, the songs of mockingbirds,
or the stories that seem twenty

generations removed from certain
possibilities of baseball or World
War I.

Chilocco Beats Kendall

Yellow Horse, Indian Twirler Was a Complete Puzzle

ARKANSAS CITY, April 18—Henry Kendall College of Tulsa, Okla. was shut out by 5 to 0 by the nine of the Chilocco Indians at Chilocco today. Yellow Horse's pitching featured.

The Daily Oklahoman, 19 April 1917

YellowHorse's World War I service records

Stitches and Hills:
(Minor League) Baseball and Pawnee, Oklahoma

THE SLOPE OF A MOUND MIGHT BE SACRED LANDSCAPE. AND SOONER OR later, sometime in mid-August maybe, when the temp reaches 100° for the fourteenth day in a row, a body begins to sweat, (even) before the sun brings a shine to the skin.

This is Pawnee, Oklahoma, and light brown grass dried to the hills. Everyone believes that shade is a precious commodity, and then there's the dust settling all over 1920. A wet handkerchief as necessary as ice crackling in lemonade, and nothing cools the air. Once in a while these foothills of the Ozarks shimmer, & the land curving moans. Cats sleep under porches, let spiders scurry by without danger or a swat. Electric and handheld fans sing and move in unison, the pitch of motors humming all through town and across the countryside. Sometimes a bed in the middle of a field, and mosquito netting thrown over a branch. Loaves of bread cheaper than a drink of water.

The swimming hole north of town is no place to court anymore, with all its old men and women and mumbled damns under the breath. It's a wonder that anything gets done—newspapers printed, groceries delivered, meals cooked, lumber cut, trash hauled, houses built. Who's got the energy to say good morning? But kids keep growing, playing rough on the hills. And by now the heat's as heavy as an iron; it might as well be God's own warm breath. And someone is surely stuck in a daydream named Alaska. Just once it'd be nice to consider a milk shake and waterfalls.

There might be a hundred people now lowering their bodies into a tub. All the trees trying to sway some motion out of the air. A little wind between the limbs. & in the middle of it all, there's talk about the young Moses YellowHorse. That fastball and his name in all the papers. Some of the boys take time to chew a little baseball beside the peanut barrel. And Mose's doing just fine after shaking that summer flu. & maybe one of them begins to say *major leagues*, nearly thinking it loud enough for the others to hear. So they all start to nodding without knowing why. Someone finally says *Little Rock's a good start before facing the likes of Babe Ruth.*

They all nod again before heading to lunch. And maybe Yel- lowHorse is perched atop a mound in New Orleans, a few stray clouds wandering in front of the sun. It could be a full-count fast- ball right down the pipe, and another hitter tossing his bat in disgust. (& he doesn't know it, but he's not losing another game all year. He doesn't know about the Dixie League Series or a major league contract—just a few weeks away.)

For now, it's a season in the bushes, and train rides from Little Rock to Birmingham to Memphis and Atlanta. It means hot plate spe- cials and a handful of other Indians on the team. The sideways glances of other patrons and short-order cooks. The way the wait- ress asks *You boys Mexican, or what?* And just once, Joe Guyon 'd like to curl his fist upside their expressions. & the locals always seem a little surprised to learn that the Little Rock club keeps at least four Indians (maybe more) on the roster.

Someone in *The Sporting News* says that all "[these] aborigines on one team is about as strong as any club ever went, but then we are right here on the [Oklahoma] border and ought to pick them up if anyone does." And an illustrator (for the same magazine) is com- pelled to draw something like:

Courtesy of *The Sporting News*, 1920

And sometimes there are scenes at hotel check-in counters. A clerk
who mumbles *I'd swear that one of them was a colored.*

While out on the field, it's any number of fans who *Woo-woo-woo-
woo-woo-woo-woo* just for "fun." And someone who'd yell *I'd rather
be dead than Red* for the first time. So YellowHorse puts his attention to pitching. Maybe he wipes a sleeve across the forehead, these
uniforms hotter than hell, and a ladle of water riding down the
neck & back between innings. And these fields, the diamonds, half-
parched from the humidity, spots where the grass goes bare. Night
baseball yet to be implemented.

In a room, later, it might be Bill Wano telling Mose, *Let their words
go by without stopping at your ears.* But something says *give 'em one hit
'n tight for Ma & Pa & all the others.* For now, it's one day after
another, weeks on the road, weeks in Little Rock. Baseball & epi-
thets during the day, stories at night.

Either dusty/dry or humid & wet, always rutted roads or clacking
rails passing under foot. Time to sleep between towns. Sometimes
an exhibition game, those local so-and-sos, some tweener-burg, and
a little extra dough in the pocket. It's always the same, semipro

boys with something to prove, and batters in rage or fear, eyes tight or wide, never knowing what to do with their mouths. And when it's done, there's the man who says *That's some arm you've got, big league worthy, and I'd know since I once faced* _____ (some Hall of Fame Pitcher).

You get all kinds in the Southern Association: the ones on their way up, on their way down, or just staying put. Guys between jobs. Guys running from wives or kids, both; maybe young enough to be running from home. And the money's just good enough to sidestep being poor. Maybe good enough for a new suit and shirts. Shoes shining like glass, and a toothpick after bacon and eggs. An hour or two early to the park. Always a tip to learn, and the ball, tiny as an acorn, lost in his hand. Sometimes a kid who asks *Where you from?* followed by *How 'bout your autograph then, Mister?*

It's the circle, the mound, wind up, and release. Bad luck to touch the base path on your way to the dugout. No one around speaks Pawnee. And the season's long. Another start later this week. Just once, it'd be nice to see zeros across the board, some kind of no-hitter. Hear a voice from home, the way light comes over the trees along Black Bear Creek, even if it's all clouds and crows.

Pawnee, Oklahoma, ca. 1920

The Big Time Begins

I N ARKANSAS AND OKLAHOMA, ONE OF THE TOP STORIES OF 1920, AS (IT might have been) revealed in (these fictional) newspaper headlines and story, concerned a sports-related matter that had the citizenry in both Little Rock and Pawnee buzzing:

"Arkansas Travelers Capture First Southern Association Title!"
—The Little Rock Journal

"Pawnee YellowHorse Comes Through! A Chief in the Making!"
—The Tulsa Dispatch

"Holy Moses! The Travelers Clinch!"
—The Pawnee Courier & Review

LITTLE ROCK, Ark., Sept. 4—For the first time in the team's twenty year stint, the Little Rock club today captured the Southern Association title. Fans were said to be sharing their jubilation all through town. Featured performances including pitchers YellowHorse and Smith, centerfielder Bing Miller, first baseman Wano, and catcher Tony Brottem. From a slow beginning early on, "Kid" Elberfeld successfully guided his team through the schedule, culminating in the final outcome. He is now getting his troops ready to face the winner of the Texas League in the Dixie League Series. All are said to be ready and excited.

The Oklahoma Sporting Report, 1920

By the time the Arkansas Travelers won their first Southern Association title in 1920, discussions about YellowHorse's hard throwing had occurred, no doubt, in various offices throughout the major leagues. Major league scouts had undoubtedly watched him pitch against other would-be or former big league players and gotten the word back to owners and managers. Their telegrams full of exclamations: *Discovered new prospect! Amazing Arm! Fastball you have to hear to believe!* A flurry of dots and dashes flying east of the Mississippi.

YellowHorse's climb to minor league baseball prominence reached its first apex when he pitched to a 21-7 record for the Little Rock club. Before that, he posted a record of 17 wins to 0 defeats in 1917 with Chilocco Indian School; then, after signing with the Des Moines Boosters of the Western League, he tossed only four innings before the league folded operations because of the World War. After playing semipro ball in Oklahoma in 1919, YellowHorse spent the winter and early spring of 1920 working in Pawnee. He then received a contract to play with Little Rock. He had no knowledge of its coming. He had no knowledge of any Little Rock scout watching him pitch. Enclosed with the contract was enough money to purchase a train ticket from Pawnee to Little Rock and a detailed map outlining directions from the Little Rock train depot to the Travelers' offices. (Lore has it that Bill Wano, a teammate of YellowHorse's at Chilocco, urged the Little Rock club to sign the hurler, as they started the season short on pitching.)

Under the guidance of the Travelers' manager, Kid Elberfeld, YellowHorse improved his mid-season record of 7 and 7 and went on to earn fourteen consecutive wins as the Travelers played in the inaugural Dixie League Series against Fort Worth, the champions of the Texas League. Though Arkansas lost the series four games to two, YellowHorse earned both of the Travelers' victories. In some ways, his one season with Little Rock proved to be his most satisfying as a professional. It represented a moment of professional youthfulness, when both YellowHorse's talents and demeanor were unblemished, either by the rigors of the majors or by professional disappointment.

In 1920, the Travelers' roster included several Indians; along with YellowHorse, they included Joe Guyon (White Earth Anishinaabe), Bill Wano (Potawatomi), and Luther "Casey" Smith (Covelo-Round Valley). Guyon, who played outfield, gained prominence as a college football star with Carlisle (in 1911 and 1912) and later with Georgia Tech (in 1917 and 1918). He'd taken up professional baseball until the fall of 1920, when the National Football League began its first season. During his professional football career, he played with the Canton Bulldogs (where he teamed up with Thorpe), the Oorang Indians, Kansas City Cowboys, and New York Giants. He eventually earned induction into the Pro Football Hall of Fame in 1966. Bill Wano, who manned first base, knew of YellowHorse as a result of their playing together at Chilocco. Finally, Luther "Casey" Smith played pitcher and joined the team late.

The regular lineup of the Travelers included the following:

c:	Tony Brottem	p:	Mose YellowHorse
1b:	Bill Wano	p:	Luther "Casey" Smith
2b:	Distel	of:	Joe Guyon
ss:	McGinnis	of:	Morrow
3b:	"Scrappy" Moore	m:	"Kid" Elberfeld
lf:	Frierson	rf:	Harper
cf:	"Bing" Miller		

During the course of the season, YellowHorse orchestrated a successful campaign. His numbers go something like this: 46 games, winning 21 and losing 7—a percentage of 75 (best in the Southern Association); he allowed 115 runs in 278 innings (an earned-run average of 3.72), striking out 138 and walking 55 batters. His work helped the team achieve an 88-59 record, which means YellowHorse won 24 precent of the team's games.

Travelers' manager Kid Elberfeld, for his part, compared Yellow-Horse's fastball to the best pitchers in the game. By doing as much, Elberfeld became instrumental in helping YellowHorse gain the attention of major league scouts. In fact, under Elberfeld's guidance, YellowHorse blossomed into a pitcher of major league caliber. Elberfeld, whose full name was Norman Arthur "The Tabasco Kid" Elberfeld, managed the Travelers in 1920 after a major league career that spanned fourteen years, from 1898 to 1914. He played with six teams, including Philadelphia's National League team, the Cincinnati Reds, the Detroit Tigers, the New York Highlanders (Yankees), the Washington Senators, and the Brooklyn Robins (Dodgers). He spent most of his career with a poor-playing New York team and in 1908 managed the ball club for 98 games; his .276 "winning" percentage still ranks among the worst of all time. He played primarily at shortstop and in 1293 games hit .271. Like another central figure in YellowHorse's baseball career, Elberfeld was a sprightly 5'7" and weighed 158 pounds. His baseball knowledge, coupled with a devotion to his players, allowed Elberfeld to send any number of minor league players on to success, whether in the major leagues or later in life.

The likes of Elberfeld, YellowHorse, Wano, "Scrappy" Moore, and Harper entertained the Little Rock fans as never before. The 1920 season would be the first time in team history that such success had been achieved. From 1901, when the organization began operations, to 1966, when it joined the Texas League, the club won only three Southern Association championships—in '20, '37, and '60. What happened in 1920, then, was cause for celebration for both the Travelers' organization and their fans: parades and salutations, dinner on the house for players and their wives. The euphoria tickled all involved. Even when the team lost the first Dixie Series to Fort Worth, the disappointment didn't hinder feelings of pride in the team's thrilling season-long journey, which had engaged the entire Little Rock community. But, as is the case with most successful minor league teams, those players who achieved notoriety quickly moved on to higher levels. Such was the case with YellowHorse. In mid-September, the news came that the Pittsburgh Pirates had expressed interest in obtaining his services.

**YELLOWHORSE IS
SIGNED BY CORSAIRS**
LITTLE ROCK, Ark., Sept. 16—
Sale of Pitcher Moses YellowHorse
to the Pittsburgh Nationals was
announced by the Little Rock club
of the Southern Association today.
Yellow horse, a full blooded Pawnee
Indian is 19 [sic] years old. He has
been the pitching sensation of the
Southern Association, having won
21 games and lost seven.
Courtesy *of The Sporting News,* 1920

This news, no doubt, caused great excitement for YellowHorse, for both the Pawnee Indian and non-Indian communities, for people in Little Rock, and for Elberfeld. Those in Little Rock, however, must have been a bit disheartened when they learned of YellowHorse's departure, realizing that one of their best players would not be returning.

Rising Through the Ranks:
From the Minors to Major Leagues—Conducting Drafts

And so it follows that: everyone conceded that the primary purpose of minor league clubs was to provide an ongoing supply of players to the majors.... Minor leagues were already in place when the National Agreement was entered into in 1903, and they continued in existence throughout the twentieth century.... The years before World War I represented the high point of the minors, in terms of the number of leagues in operation.... In 1912 over forty minor leagues existed, but the number had fallen to nine in 1918.

The entrepreneurial motives of minor league club owners were many and varied, but the value of their franchises was decisively affected by the value of their players. Although some minor league teams drew well at the gate, the largest share of their revenues came ... from the sale of their players to major league clubs... Both the minor and major leagues, then, had an overriding common goal ... of funneling players from the minors to the majors, which was facilitated by a "minor league draft."

From the early twentieth century on, the minor leagues had been divided into classified levels of franchises, allegedly approximating the caliber of play in a given minor league. The classifications were designed to facilitate player development, but they also served to establish compensation rules for drafted players and limits on the number of players that could be drafted. In 1911 an agreement was reached dividing the minors into AA, A, B, C, and D-level leagues, fixing compensation levels [depending on a player's league level] ... and limiting the capacity of the majors to draft more than a designated number of players from the higher minor leagues (only one player per team from AA clubs).

[It should come as no surprise, then, that] minor league players were to minor league cities as big-leaguers were to cities of the majors: familiar figures with whom one could identify and for whom one could root. [And when] a major league team bought one of those players, his departure was typically a civic loss. (278-80, 290)

—G. Edward White, *Creating the National Pastime: Baseball Transforms Itself, 1903-1953*

Courtesy of Bob Lemke

1922 trading card

This is the only major league baseball card made of YellowHorse. It was issued by the Exhibit Supply Company. Some dealers have appraised the card at over $1,700.

Some Show

LO, THE INDIAN REAPPEARS

1921 photograph of YellowHorse, which appeared in
The Sporting News's *"Spring Training Report"*

The Meaning of P, or What It Means to Wear #50 (for the Pittsburgh Pirates)

This moment begins in the dim light
Of a locker room, and Mose Yellow-
Horse struggling against his uniform

Buttons. *It's just y'r nerves* the boys
Tell him, but he knows it's butterflies
And the sparkle of Opening Day.

Soon enough he'll take in the field,
The crowd of twenty-five thousand,
See mustard dripping from the chins

Of enchanted fathers.

This will be the first time they've seen
An Indian in Pittsburgh. And some
Whoop and holler; mumble & inquire.

Some will cheer. They watch the Reds
And Pirates battle deep into the tussle;
Tip and tuck from the start.

It's April 21, and Mose YellowHorse
Doesn't know that kids are peeking
Through cracks in the outfield wall.

He can't hear them asking *Who's that
Number 50?* Instead, he's got his eyes
On the curve of a catcher's mitt, his

Face covered in the shade of his cap.
And he doesn't know that the pop
Of his fastball has an echo that reaches

Press Row.

When he enters the game in the top
Of the sixth, it's tied at six apiece.
And some numerists might've said

That means something ominous, but
YellowHorse listens to the cheers of
All the clubhouse joes, something like

Go get 'em Chief.

He jogs from the bullpen to
the mound, where the twist
And turn of his body resembles

Dance. After his first pitch, he will
Smile at the sound of *Stee-rike one.*
His mates in the field yell *Atta boy.*

And the headlines on April 22 read
Indian Twirler Works Medicine on Reds.
Baseball writers will say *YellowHorse is*

The latest idol of the Smoky City fans.
History says he is the first Pirate
Rookie to win a home opener.

After the game is over, his teammates
Say *Have another, Mosey, ol' boy.* He'll
Walk home at 3 a.m. with the faces

Of twenty-five thousand on his mind,
And he doesn't care about the climb
To his apartment, or the hum of hall-

Way lights. It's eggs over easy. One,
Two, three strikes, you're out. A perfect
Career record. And *P* is for Pawnee.

*   *   *

Box score of YellowHorse's first major league win:

Pirates Trim Reds

Open Home Season by Capturing Nip-and-Tuck Contest, 8 to 7.

PITTSBURGH, April 21—Pittsburgh opened the local season today with a victory over Cincinnati by a score of 8 to 7. The game was tip and tuck from start to finish, the winning runs coming in the eighth inning. Adams started to pitch for Pittsburgh, but was hit hard and gave way to Ponder in the third, who was forced out of the box because of the visitors' heavy hitting in the sixth inning, YellowHorse finishing the game.

The score:

PITTSBURGH

	Ab	R	H	Po	A
Bigbee, lf	3	2	2	3	1
Carey, cf	3	1	0	2	0
Maranv'le, ss	4	2	3	3	3
Cutshaw, 2b	4	1	2	3	3
Whitted, rf	2	0	0	2	0
Tierney, 3b	4	0	2	2	0
Grimm, 1b	4	1	1	8	0
Schmidt, c	3	1	1	4	1
Adams, p	0	0	0	0	0
Ponder, p	2	0	0	0	1
Yellowh'se, p	1	0	0	0	1
Total	30	8	11	27	12

CINCINNATI

	Ab	R	H	Po	A
Paskert, cf	5	1	2	3	0
Daubert, 1b	4	0	2	6	0
Bohne, 3b	5	1	1	1	2
Duncan, lf	5	3	3	4	0
Bressler, rf	4	1	4	1	0
Fonseca, 2b	5	0	0	3	1
Crane, ss	5	0	1	2	1
Wingo, c	4	0	1	4	3
Napier, p	2	1	1	0	0
Brenton, p	1	0	0	0	2
Marquard, p	0	0	0	0	1
Total	36	7	15	24	10

Pittsburgh...2 0 0 1 3 0 0 2 x–8
Cincinnati...0 1 3 0 0 2 1 0 0–7

Errors—Carey, Schmidt, Fonseca
Two-base hit—Duncan. Three-base hits—Duncan (2), Napier, Maranville, Cutshaw, Grimm, Tierney. Stolen bases—Bohne. Sacrifice—Daubert, Fonseca, Crane, Whitted (2). Double plays—Maranville, Cutshaw and Grimm, Cutshaw and Grimm. Left on bases Cincinnati 6, Pittsburgh 2. Base on balls—Off Brenton 2, YellowHorse 1. Hits—Off Napier 8 in 4 1-3 Innings, Brenton 3 in 5 1-3, Marquard 0 in 1-3, Adams 7 in 2 1-3, Ponder 4 in 3, YellowHorse 4 in 3 2-3. Struck out—By Napier 4, Adams 1. Winning pitcher—YellowHorse. Losing pitcher—Brenton. Umpires—Quigley and O'Day. Time of game—1:57.

New York Times, 22 April 1921

1921 & Other Numbers

YELLOWHORSE'S ROOKIE SEASON CAME TO AN ABRUPT END ON JULY 5 when he sustained an injury during a game against St. Louis, a game that he lost. Shortly afterward, he underwent surgery to correct the problem. In a letter dated July 12, S. W. Dreyfuss, the Pirates' treasurer, wrote to Mr. C. E. Vandervoort, a prominent Pawnee merchant:

> Dear Sir:
> You have probably seen in the papers that Moses Yellow Horse underwent an operation a few days ago. At his request I am writing to advise that there is nothing seriously the matter with "The Chief". During a recent game he strained a ligament and our doctor felt that unless there was an operation to relieve the trouble Yellow Horse would be useless to our club for the balance of the season. The operation was entirely successful. The patient is already sitting up and will leave the hospital in another week.
> Very truly yours,
> S. W. Dreyfuss (signed)
> Treasurer

Unfortunately for YellowHorse and the Pirates, his pitching services were lost for the balance of the season, and he ended his rookie campaign with a 5-3 record and an earned run average of 2.98. The breakdown of his wins and losses is as follows:

April 21	vs. Cincinnati	(W)	8-7	in Pittsburgh
May 30	vs. Chicago (N)	(W)	6-3	in Pittsburgh
June 7	vs. Boston (N)	(L)	10-7	in Pittsburgh
June 16	vs. Brooklyn	(W)	6-5 (in 17)	in Pittsburgh
June 20	vs. Philadelphia (N)	(W)	3-2	in Pittsburgh
June 25	vs. St. Louis (N)	(L)	7-4	in St. Louis
June 30	vs. Cincinnati	(W)	5-3	in Pittsburgh
July 5	vs. St. Louis	(L)	8-2	in Pittsburgh

Aside from the Pirates' home opener, one of the more exciting games for YellowHorse came against Philadelphia on June 20, a contest he started and won, 3 to 2. In eight innings of work, Yel-lowHorse allowed only two runs (both in the eighth) and struck out seven men in the process. During the game, he entertained not only Pirate fans but also Baseball Commissioner Kennesaw Mountain Landis who attended the game with team owner Barney Dreyfuss. The day after this contest, YellowHorse, Landis, and Barney Dreyfuss sat down together for a Q & A session in order for Landis to meet and speak with the Pirates' newest acquisition. According to William Jakub, Landis's fascination with YellowHorse was so great that the new commissioner requested the meeting. Afterward, "Landis was impressed with the Pirates' latest acquisition" (188).

As the season progressed, however, YellowHorse could do nothing but encourage his Pirate teammates while his injury healed. While he sat in the clubhouse after August, YellowHorse watched the Pirates battle the New York Giants in a heated pennant race. Both teams stayed within three to five games of one another for most of the season, and by September, Pittsburgh had a four-game lead heading into a series at the Polo Grounds. Too full of confidence, a few Pirate players predicted that the pennant was theirs, that they would take two of five games to wrap up the National League championship. Unfortunately for the Pirates, the Giants swept the series. The Pirates, bruised egos and all, then went on to finish the season four games behind the Giants.

Because of their strong but disappointing season, the Pirates earned a $21,939.17 share of the World Series with their second-

1921 Pirate Regulars:	
1B	Grimm
2B	Cutshaw
SS	Maranville
3B	Barnhart
RF	Whitted
CF	Carey
LF	Bigbee
C	Schmidt
P	Cooper
P	Glazner
P	Hamilton
P	Adams
P	Morrison
P	Zinn
P	Carlson
P	YellowHorse

place finish. For his part, YellowHorse received a full share of
$839.97. In a letter to Pawnee merchant Vandervoort, Leslie M.
O'Connor, the secretary-treasurer of major league baseball, wrote
on December 6, 1921,

> Dear Sir:
>   In accordance with your letter of November 30th to Commis-
> sioner Landis, I enclose a copy of a circular letter sent to all
> Pittsburgh players, including Moses YellowHorse.
>   As I recall it, he was listed to receive two-thirds of a share in
> the recommendation submitted by Captain Carey. You will note
> that this has been increased by the Commissioner to a full share.
> Very truly yours,
Leslie M. O'Connor (signed)
Secretary-Treasurer

A quick glance at Captain Max Carey's original recommenda-
tion shows that YellowHorse was to receive a full share, as voted by
his teammates. O'Connor, for some reason, was mistaken about
how much YellowHorse's Pirate teammates wanted to give him.

He also received a hero's welcome when he returned to Pawnee
at the end of the season. So many hands to shake. Some odd jobs
around town, working construction, putting his Chilocco-learned
carpentry skills to use. There were functions to attend, dates with
young Pawnee women. And stories; there were so many stories to
tell: the one about waking up in a tub full of warm shaving cream,
and how the hotel owner in Chicago cursed in Italian when he saw
the mess. Maybe YellowHorse showed off the scar from his surgery;
he got more wounds throwing a baseball than serving in the War.

Eight to Five

"What this country needs is some more ballplayers like Moses YellowHorse and his roommate, the Rabbit [Walter Maranville]."
—Pat Harmon, *Cincinnati Post & Times Star*, 24 April 1964

THE PIRATES' 1922 SEASON, LIKE THE YEAR BEFORE, LOOKED PROMISING. Many sports writers in their spring training reports tabbed Pittsburgh as one of the top teams in the National League. And Pittsburgh manager George Gibson had every reason to believe the club would build on the previous year's experience and finish the season stronger than in '21. Gibson hoped a few changes in the Pirate lineup might improve the team's offense. Since the Pirates finished 1921 batting .285, fourth worst in the league, Gibson figured to remedy the problem with some stronger batters. Changes were made at second and third bases, in right field, and at catcher. The most prominent of these substitutions was Pie Traynor taking over third base in place of Clyde Barnhart, who batted .258 in 1921. Traynor hit at a .282 clip and drove in 81 runs—a solid rookie year for the future Hall-of-Famer—and brought much more offensive production to third base. Other switches included Cotton Tierney for George Cutshaw at second base, Reb Russell for Possom Whitted in right field, and Johnny Gooch at catcher for Wally Schmidt. With so many changes among the day-to-day Pirate regulars, other National League pitchers were unfamiliar with certain batters' tendencies. As a result, the 1922 Pirates led the league in hitting with a .308 average.

Unfortunately, the Pirates' pitchers didn't hold up their end of the bargain, and the hitters' bats didn't start igniting until the end of June. The Pirate twirlers as a staff, which gave up a stingy 3.17 runs in 1921, allowed 3.98 runs in '22. As a result, Pittsburgh stumbled out of the gate to a 32-33 record, which cost George Gibson his job. He resigned in June, and Bill "Deacon" McKechnie took over the managerial duties. Team owner Barney Dreyfuss demanded that McKechnie get control of the players, as the pervading perception was that Gibson treated his players softly and let them break certain team policies without penalty. Dreyfuss specifically pointed out two players—YellowHorse and Maranville—as the primary offenders. McKechnie's solution to the problem was to room with YellowHorse and Maranville when the team was on the road.

An Interview with Babe Adams

BABE ADAMS (1882-1968) PLAYED NINETEEN YEARS IN THE MAJORS, ONE year with the St. Louis Nationals (1906) and the other eighteen with the Pittsburgh Pirates (1907, 1909-1916, and 1918-1926). During his tenure with the Pirates, he pitched in almost five hundred games, and in 1909 and 1925 he helped the team win the World Series. In 1960, Adams returned to Pittsburgh as the team's guest to watch the Pirates compete against the Yankees in the World Series. He spoke about his days with the team, about his early days in baseball, and about some of the raucous characters with whom he played, including Mose YellowHorse and Rabbit Maranville. As Adams, then seventy-eight years old, recalled his experiences, he spoke eloquently with his subtle Hoosier drawl in the hotel restaurant, where he was talking over old times with some friends. What follows is an excerpt from the *Pittsburgh Journal & News*.

PJN: What did you enjoy about your playing days in Pittsburgh?

Adams: I liked getting to know ballplayers from all over different parts of the country. Every spring there'd be new guys from places I'd never heard of—small towns in Idaho, or Florida, or Texas, even Canada. I'd meet guys from Georgia or Alabama and couldn't hardly understand 'em at first. Guys from up in New England were just as hard too. But once I got to know them, they were usually good guys. All just trying to play some baseball and travel around the country.

PJN: Which year was the most disappointing to you? Which season upset you more than any other?

Adams: Well, 1921 was a big disappointment. Poor Gibby, I still feel sorry for him. He was the team's manager at the time, and he took it awful hard—the way we folded like a pup tent down the stretch. We had a comfortable lead late in the season, and going into a series with the Giants in New York we got swept. They just mauled us. We were devastated. Lost the pennant by four games. 'Course it didn't help that some of our players were saying how we were going to do this and do that to beat the Giants. That just made them all hell bent on whipping us. And they did. Out hit, out pitched, out fielded us. In all ways they demolished us. Then they went on and beat the Yankees in the Series.

PJN: Who were the players that talked about beating the Giants?

Adams: Well, no one ever said who they were in the newspapers, but I heard it was Rabbit Maranville, shooting off his mouth, the way he always did. That was just his way. Supposedly, Barney Dreyfuss, he owned the club, fined Rabbit for telling reporters what we were going to do to the Giants. If you know John McGraw at all, you know he told his players what So-and-so from the Pirates said they were going to do to his team. I heard that Dreyfuss fined Rabbit his whole World Series share. That would've been over eight hundred bucks. And I don't have to tell you how much more money that was in 1921 than it is now.

PJN: What other crazy things happened back then? It seems a lot of ballplayers were pretty wild. Players like Babe Ruth and Rabbit Maranville, of course, behaved in a more reckless manner than today's players. Is that true?

Adams: Since I haven't spent a lot of time around today's players, I can't really say if they're crazier acting than players back then. I am sure that Rabbit Maranville was the wildest piece of baseball player I ever saw. In Pittsburgh, I think he was with the team for four years, he teamed up with this pitcher named YellowHorse. Moses was his name. We called him Chief since he was an Indian. He made the team in '21 and everyone was real surprised. We all thought he was gonna come to spring training then go back to the bushes. But he had a fastball with more gas than Texaco. And Gibby just couldn't let the guy go. I remember this one time; I'm getting back to your question. It was in '22, and Gibby had just resigned from the team. This would've been in June. And 'Deacon' McKechnie just took over managing the team. Barney Dreyfuss told him to keep a look out for Maranville and YellowHorse. I heard that Dreyfuss called 'em both wild Indians, and he wanted to make sure they stayed in line. So Deacon decided to bunk with Rabbit and the Chief when the team's on the road. We all warned him to be careful. But he wouldn't listen. (Mr. Adams pauses and breaks a slight smile. He takes a sip of coffee.)

PJN: And . . . so? *(He nods.)*

Adams: It became known as "The Pigeon Affair of 1922." And it was in New York. What happened was that the Chief and Rabbit made a bet to see who could catch the most pigeons bare-handed. To make it fun, they decided to do their pigeon catching from a sixteenth-story ledge at the hotel where we were staying.

PJN: That's pretty stupid.

Adams: You just had to know 'em. Rabbit was this half-pint of explosive wildness from Springfield, Massachusetts. He probably stood about 5'5". Didn't weigh any more than a slice of bread in a paper sack. And next to Rabbit, the Chief looked like he might've been half-brother to a sycamore tree. He came up from Oklahoma, from one of those tribes. From near Tulsa, I remember him saying. He wasn't that tall; really about my size. But he had an arm. And the two of them together made lots of excitement, always kept Barney Dreyfuss worrying.

PJN: What exactly did they bet?

Adams: Well, you know those two; they were always looking to cure a calm night. And Rabbit said to YellowHorse, "I'm sure I can beat you at this game we played as kids back in Springfield." He went on and told Chief about it, how they'd try to catch birds barehanded, and the bet was on. They went and got a bag of pop-corn, I think it was, and started laying kernels out on the ledge. Chief was out there, still in his suit, and good thing it wasn't a windy night. He was out there trying to charm the birds, and pretty soon he caught himself a handful. Then Rabbit went out there and I guess he started dancing around, acting like some ballerina. And when his time was up he had eight birds.

PJN: So Maranville won the contest then, and what prize did he get?

Adams: Well, Rabbit was kind enough to share his 80-proof winnings with ol' Mosey boy.

PJN: What did McKechnie do when he found out?

Adams: Thing is, he wouldn't 've had any idea. He was out having dinner with John McGraw. He didn't know what they were up to. When he got back to the hotel room around ten o'clock, he was surprised and happy to find both of 'em sleeping. He figured he caught a break since he didn't have to go looking for them, like usual. Then he opened his closet door to hang up his coat. Started reaching for a hanger. But he got a face full of pigeons. They were flying right for his head, and he ducked. Rabbit told me that the Deacon hit the floor so loud it must've startled God.

PJN: What'd McKechnie do?

Adams: We all heard that stirring down the hall, and we shot up to see what all the commotion was. On my way to the room I saw the Deacon walking away real quick. I went in the room and saw pigeons flying all around. Rabbit and the Chief were on their beds just rolling and laughing. I mean they're in their pajamas. And Max Carey was in there too. He was smiling and trying to grab the pigeons and let them out the window. He was saying "we need to get these birds outta here." At one point, I think someone said "anyone gotta gun," and that kept us stirring for another twenty minutes. Their room was full till midnight. And we got a real kick out of their prank. After that, the Deacon was one of the boys. 'Course he didn't room with them ever again. And it took him awhile, but he finally learned to laugh about it.

PJN: What did he do to Maranville and YellowHorse then?

Adams: Oh, he fined them. And Barney Dreyfuss called them both into his office when we returned to Pittsburgh. But the team was so excited about what happened that we got on such a good winning streak we actually competed for the pennant. If those two rascals had spent their time thinking about baseball all of the time, instead of half of it, then we could've played in another World Series or two.

1922 Pirates lineup:

1B	Grimm
2B	Tierney*
SS	Maranville
3B	Traynor*
RF	Russell*
CF	Carey
LF	Bigbee
C	Gooch*
P	Cooper
P	Morrison
P	Glazner
P	Adams
P	Hamilton
P	Carlson
P	YellowHorse

new player

A Bean for the (Georgia) Peach:
The Detroit Incident

A report in the September 27, 1922 *New York Times* put it this way:

> **TY COBB IS INJURED**
> **Tigers' Manager Hit by Pitched Ball**
> **in Exhibition With Pirates**
>
> DETROIT, Sept. 26—Ty Cobb was hit by
> a pitched ball thrown by YellowHorse
> and was carried from the field in the
> fifth inning of today's exhibition game
> with the Pittsburgh Nationals, which
> Detroit won, 5 to 4. Cobb was batting
> for Cole, the ball striking him on the leg.
> Cole and Ehmke held the Pirates to four
> hits, all of which were for extra bases.

Seventy years later, in June 1992, Pawnee tribal member Norman Rice spoke to me about this incident. He invited me into his
small bungalow in Pawnee, and we talked about YellowHorse's
career with the Pirates. Rice, a wiry man whose face and body were
toughened by years spent working outdoors, spoke his stories with
a soft elegance. Though some of his words could be difficult to
understand, he was as kind, gentle, and willing to share his stories
with me as anyone in Pawnee. When speaking of YellowHorse's
experience in Detroit, he said:

> Ty Cobb was crowding the plate anyway, he always did. And
> Mose wasn't going to let him get away with it. Cobb was up there
> yelling all kinds of Indian prejudice, real mean slurs at Mose, just
> making him mad anyway. So he shakes off four pitches until the
> catcher gives him the fastball sign, and Mose nods his head. I
> mean everyone in Detroit was whooping and all that silliness. So
> he winds up and fires the ball as hard as he could, and he
> knocked Cobb right in the head, right between the eyes. Mose

knocked him cold. And a fight nearly broke out at home plate. All the Tigers' players came rushing off the bench. The Pirate players started running toward Mose. But no punches were thrown. They just carried Ty Cobb off the field. And all three of the Pirates' outfielders just stood together in center and laughed. Said they wished they could see it again.

And still another account in a March 1994 issue of *The Bleacher Bum* stated:

On Sept. 26, YellowHorse was called upon to pitch against the Detroit Tigers in an exhibition game at Detroit. In a 5-4 loss he plunked Ty Cobb so severely that the Georgia Peach had to be carried off the field.   *Courtesy of Bob Lemke*

. . .

Of these three accounts, the most engaging and descriptive is Norman Rice's, who heard the story from YellowHorse in all likelihood. Where the two newspaper accounts offer factual and bare-bones information, Rice's story contains an intriguing subplot that addresses tensions between Indians and Euroamericans. In a reversal of the all-too-familiar narrative, it is YellowHorse who holds the weapon (a wicked fastball) and inflicts harm. For YellowHorse to level one of the most hated (white) ballplayers in baseball history lends an ironic twist to the story. The empowered Indian dares to make his feelings public and retaliates against Cobb, his teammates, and the Detroit fans, when he disobeys the Pirates' catcher and chooses to throw a fastball at the ridiculing batter. That YellowHorse's teammates support his actions, as Norman Rice's narrative shows, clearly suggests their loyalty to him as a teammate. They rally to his defense in a hostile environment and protect him from revenge-minded Detroit players and fans. In the same way that the 1947 Brooklyn Dodger players finally supported

Jackie Robinson, the same kind of team-first spirit takes hold in the 1922 Pittsburgh clubhouse. A Hall-of-Fame player like Rabbit Maranville, though no imposing physical specimen, probably stuck his nose into the fray. In fact, it's not too difficult to imagine Maranville leading the defensive charge. It's not too difficult to imagine him standing protectively in front of the much bigger YellowHorse. And it's not too difficult to imagine lots of people laughing after the fact.

A Bean for the Peach: Counting Coup

Moments of Pawnee, Oklahoma,
can drift by at ninety miles

per hour, even in late September,
even when the red hand-sewn

seams of a baseball spin like fancy
dancing.

     • • •

At the same time, moments of Narrows,
Georgia, can stand as firm as trees

in an orchard, even when an Indian's
heater comes along in late September.

In the hands of an able hitter, a sturdy
Louisville Slugger can stare down

any fastball west of the mighty
Mississip.

     • • •

And moments of Detroit, Michigan,
can jeer as loud, say, as a cavalry

stampede, even in 1922, even
when it's Tiger Stadium and a game

that means nothing in the standings.

.   .   .

& so it goes, sooner rather than later,
the bean (ball) flying from Mose

YellowHorse's hand will catch up
with Ty Cobb's peach.

And all the smart ass in the world
won't protect Cobb's face from

Pawnee intentions.

.   .   .

And someone's dad once said:
"You mess with the bull, you

get the horn."

.   .   .

When YellowHorse heard
the whoops and hollers

of Cobb & all Detroit,
he reared back on his right

leg and let all of history fly
through his arm.

And somewhere in the cosmos
the moment of contact still echoes,

is still spiraling into space
with laughter following close

behind.

Picking Moments

He hears a pair of crows outside
His hotel window. A slight sample
Of truth. Fragmented voices, half-

Recalled. Down on street corners
Men ignore Prohibition, and truth
Navigates a teetering gateway. He

Is alone in his room listening for
Solutions. If he's quiet enough, he
Remembers. He can begin to untie

Stories caught in his memory. Out
Beyond the disconnection of 1922,
Baseball is perfect again.

For now, Mose YellowHorse is 24,
And that might mean he's waking
Up at eleven every morning beside

A hangover. It might mean boys
Are seeking his autograph. Maybe
He's participating in nightly rituals

Of moonshine & hootchy-kootchy.
The way it is in each town—slipping
Sideways into speakeasies, two men,

Two women at a time. A password
Whispered to a pair of shifty eyes.
A girl who says her grandma is half-

Indian. Back in Pawnee, moths are
Beating themselves against screens.
A white bead concealed from one

Hand to another.* Young men slide
The world through their fingers. On
The verge of song, a Pawnee woman

Exposes her words to a prayer about
Seeds twisting like dancers to the sun.
Maybe a father can mumble a death-

Bed speech that begins *To-mor-row.*
And sooner or later the need to walk
Saves every life from its destruction.

---

* The white bead is an allusion to the Pawnee hand game, a contest played by
young men, during which they hide a white bead in the hands of a member of
their team, or war party, while a member from an opposing team tries to determine in which hand the bead is hidden. As Gene Weltfish notes in *The Lost
Universe,* "War songs were sung and in the motioning of the hands of the line in
which the bead was hidden, the bead might be transferred by sleight of hand during the guessing" (398). In other Pawnee games, a white bead sometimes serves as
a symbol of the earth.

Ruth Versus YellowHorse

WHEN I MADE MY FIRST VISITS TO PAWNEE, I LISTENED TO STORIES AND anecdotes about YellowHorse striking out Babe Ruth. Different Pawnee tribal members continually recounted how he took down the mighty Ruth; since I planned to include the information, I was happy to come across a full account of the narrative in 1995 when Darrell Gambill, head of the Pawnee Chamber of Commerce, wrote about the situation in the January 18th edition of *The Pawnee Chief.*

It was October 2, 1922 and a great day for baseball in Drumright [Oklahoma]. Several members of the New York Yankees agreed to come. Babe Ruth would be on the Drumright team and Bob Meusel would play for the other team from Shamrock.

Hundreds of fans from surrounding towns filled the bleachers and others brought standing room only tickets to see the famous Babe Ruth in action.

The fans roared as Ruth came to bat in the first inning. The Babe responded by doffing his hat and waving. The crowd waited in anticipation. 4 pitches whistled across the plate. The Babe missed three of them and struck out. The crowd sat in silence.

But in the third inning the bases were loaded when Ruth stepped up to the plate to a great ovation. They were still with him and again he waved confidently to the fans.

He took a wicked swing at the first pitch and missed. He let a low outside pitch go by. Then he stepped up and took a vicious cut at the third pitch for strike 2. A low inside pitch brought the count to 2-2. The next pitch was a sizzler down the middle. Ruth saw it coming and swung with all his might. He didn't come close. The crowd was silent this time. They booed. There was no joy in Drumright that day. The mighty Bambino had struck out with the bases loaded. Drumright lost to Shamrock 7-5.

The fans knew the pitcher playing with Shamrock was ... Pittsburgh Pirate ... [and] Pawnee Indian ... Moses YellowHorse.

Some Trouble

Baseball card of YellowHorse with Sacramento

s Business

news came by cable, something like:
ιιαu..d to Sacramento of the Pacific Association. New manager
Charlie Pick.

But no one was there to record his reaction. Perhaps a fist
through a wall—some scar inflicted.

> Manager Bill McKechnie of the Pirates
> added to the club's payroll a right-
> handed flinger, by the name of E. D.
> Kuntz [sic], who was last year a member
> of the tail-end Sacramento Club. In addi-
> tion to $7,500 in cash the Pirates threw
> in two pitchers, one infielder, and one
> outfielder, only one of whom was an
> active member of the Pirates forces last
> season. The pitchers were Moses Yel-
> lowHorse, Indian hurler, who has held
> down the "bull-pen" assignment for two
> seasons, and Bill Hughes, former Brook-
> lyn sand-lot player, who was with the
> Rochester Club last summer. The
> infielder was Claude Rohwer, brother of
> the old White Sox star, who was on the
> rolls of the Charleston, S.C. team, and
> the outfielder, Harry Brown, who chased
> flies for the Flint, Mich., team in the
> Michigan State League in 1922.
>
> Kuntz comes to the Pirates highly
> recommended. He is a right hander and
> 23 years old. In spite of the fact that he
> was on a tail-end team last summer he
> turned in fourteen victories out of
> thirty-two starts.
>
> *New York Times*, 14 December 1922

Kunz's major league career totals:

YEAR	TEAM	W	L	PCT	ERA	G	GS	CG	IP	H	BB	SO
1923	PIT N	1	2	.333	5.52	21	2	1	45.2	48	24	12

How Many Ways an Arm Dies

Account #1

Pawnee elder Phil Gover told me this YellowHorse story during my first week in Pawnee. One early afternoon in the dining hall he spoke about YellowHorse's baseball days in California. He told me, too, that at eighty-six, he was proud to be Pawnee and proud to be a veteran of World War II. Without sharing the specific details with me, Mr. Gover said it was during the war in Germany that he lost his left arm. Though his words were sometimes difficult for me to understand, I learned to compensate by leaning forward much of the time; I now know he was employing what's called the "Gover mumble." It was apparent to me that Mr. Gover kept his sense of humor handy and spoke gently, always aiming to teach. He always welcomed me at his table.

> Mose was on his way to California, after he was traded to Sacramento. And he was sleeping on a train. He fell asleep on his right side and slept that way all night. After a while his arm started to fall asleep. When he woke up, the arm kept on sleeping. He never quite got the sleep out of his arm. It stayed there for years, the sleep did. Even later on, when he was older, he still rubbed the arm. He'd rub and rub it for hours. Funny thing is, it didn't allow him not to pitch. He could still throw a great curveball when he was fifty. One thing it did was make him do more with his left hand. It got to the point that he could throw, fish, even write with his left hand. 'Course, some people always said he could throw with his left as good as his right. He even tried it in a game once. Out in California, his team was getting beat real bad, and he threw his mitt down and started throwing left-handed. He reared back and fired a strike at the catcher. And he kept on doing it. Got all the batters out that way, the rest of the game. I guess it helped his right arm when he did that. When he came back, sometime in the mid-'20s, he did it all the time in games. It became his way of showing off. But still after every game, he'd rub his right arm.

Account #2

Bill Conlin, a longtime sports writer for the *Sacramento Bee*, spoke to me over the phone in September 1992 about Yel-lowHorse's post-Pittsburgh days. It was Conlin who, in 1958, suggested that the Sacramento ball club fly YellowHorse out to California to honor him with a "YellowHorse Night." He told me that as a little boy, he saw YellowHorse pitch for Sacramento and remembered his father telling him that YellowHorse had the best fastball he'd ever seen—that is, before he injured his arm.

It happened when Mose was pitching with the Fort Worth team in the Texas League. He liked to stay in Dallas. The action was there. So he stayed in a hotel and got rides out to the Fort Worth park. One night he's whooping it up in his room. He's all tipsy and out of control. I think his room was on the third or fourth floor. Anyway he was flirting with some girls out on the street or something, and he fell out of the window. That's right, he fell out of a window drunk. It was a story he loved to tell. He came back here in 1958. The owner of the Sacramento ball team, Sam Gordon, flew him out here and a banquet was given in his honor. Mose presented Gordon with a headdress and told all kinds of stories. He told us how he fell out the window in Dallas. He was trying to get some girls to come up to his room. Him and some other guys were up there yelling at them from the room. He leaned out the window and made a waving motion to them. When he did, he lost his balance. He fell into some wires. Telephone wires or electric wires, something like that. He bounced off the wires and slammed into the concrete. Well, he laid there for a second and didn't move. The guys he was with screamed out the window and rushed out of the room when they didn't see him move. Mose was still lying on the ground when they got downstairs. By that time, a small crowd had gathered around to see what was going on. They rolled him over and saw his arm, his pitching arm—all bloody. They got him up to the room and after a few minutes revived him. At the time he wasn't able to move his arm. "I'm crippled. I'm crippled," he screamed at his cronies. They fed him some more whiskey 'til he passed out and left him alone in his room. He told us that story in 1958. He said he couldn't ever pitch after that. I guess he was pulling our legs 'cause his arm wasn't curled up or anything. At the game in his honor, he threw a fastball that could've baffled the youngsters on the Sacramento team.

Account #3

Albin LeadingFox, also a Pawnee elder, was in 1992 the only known close relative of YellowHorse still living around Pawnee. LeadingFox, like a number of older Pawnee men I spoke with, did not talk loudly, which seemed a bit odd to me, since most other people I knew who were hard of hearing, as Mr. LeadingFox was, compensated for their "loss" by talking overly loud. Unlike Mr. Gover, who was always ready with a story, Mr. LeadingFox did not share many stories with me. Rather, he spoke in short declarative sentences and did not offer many details. After talking with Mr. LeadingFox, I realized that all the men who shared with me their stories wore baseball caps—though none of them was of the Pittsburgh Pirate variety. Mr. LeadingFox told me about YellowHorse's injury in the most succinct terms; he said:

It was the drinking. It deadened his arm.

Account #4

Mose YellowHorse, as quoted in *The Bleacher Bum* by Bob Lemke:

In the first month of the 1924 season, YellowHorse suffered a serious injury to his pitching arm. Sacramento was carrying an 18-5 lead into the bottom of the ninth inning at Salt Lake City when the home team began to rally. With cozy fences and the high altitude, the lead was by no means safe and the Solons manager Charlie Pick began going through his bullpen.

When the Bees had scored 10 runs, Pick told YellowHorse, "Warm up fast, if the next batter gets a hit, in you're going." With only three warm-up pitches, YellowHorse was called to the mound with the bases loaded, the tying run on first base. [YellowHorse] reminisced later, "I went in and I threw just nine pitches, striking out in order John Peters, Tony Lazzeri, and Duffy

Lewis," and nailing down the victory. "That was the finest job of pitching I ever did," YellowHorse said, "But I couldn't raise my arm the next day. Jack Downey was the trainer but he couldn't stop the pain."

YellowHorse apparently resorted to heavy applications of 80-proof pain relief. By mid-June, *The Sporting News* reported, "Chief Moses YellowHorse has gone the way of all bad Injuns. The Chief would not keep in condition, and was no longer of use to the team, so he was sold to Fort Worth, Texas. The Chief is his own worst enemy. He has the ability to be a big league pitcher, but lacks the inclination to keep in shape to pitch."

. . .

So it seems that YellowHorse:
   a) blew his arm out in a game versus Salt Lake in 1924
      (by his own admission), or
   b) drank his arm to death (by one account), or
   c) slept his arm to death (by one account), or
   d) fell his arm to death (by one account).
Whatever the case, there is little doubt that these various narratives have developed as alternatives to YellowHorse's account to complement other stories about his outlandish behavior as a professional ballplayer. Any story that details stress to YellowHorse's right arm finally offers as good an explanation as any other in accounting for the demise of his pitching abilities and professional baseball career. Whether it's falling from a hotel window, not taking enough time to warm up, falling asleep on the arm, or drinking too much, each narrative implies that something unfortunate (even silly, or stupid) happened to cause YellowHorse's pitching ability to wane. In each story, aside from Philip Gover's, YellowHorse had an opportunity to avoid tragedy.

   He could have, after all, quit drinking and not fallen out of a hotel window;

   He could have quit flirting with Texas girls walking the streets of Dallas;

   He could have told Charlie Pick that he wasn't warmed up and taken more time to loosen his arm;

He could have quit drinking;

He could have quit drinking.

That's the ease of hindsight. It's too easy to forget: on most of the teams with which he played, with the exception of Little Rock, he was the only Indian; he could've felt pressure from those around him and from those in Pawnee to be another "Chief" Bender.

Regardless of which account best explains the reasons for the deterioration of YellowHorse's pitching abilities, he threw his last pitch as a professional on May 1, 1926. With Omaha of the Western League, his final pitching line against Tulsa went like this:

2 & 1/3 innings pitched; gave up 6 hits and 5 runs; and lost 9-8.

Later, after he returned to Pawnee, YellowHorse spent many summer days and nights playing with semipro teams. With those clubs, in and around Pawnee, he gained celebrity status for his ambidextrous pitches, which he released from numerous angles. According to Henry Stone Road, Mose even tossed underhanded from the mound. He did this, of course, because of his arm injury. "He'd whip the ball around and the batter couldn't even see it coming," Stone Road said of YellowHorse's unorthodox delivery.

. . .

The totals of his entire professional pitching career went as follows:

YEAR	TEAM	LEAGUE	W	L	SAVE	PCT.	ERA	GAMES	GS	GC	IP	H	SO	BB
1917	Ponca C.	NA												
1918	Des M.	WL	NA								4	4		2
1919	(Semipro ball in Oklahoma)													
1920	L.R.	SA	21	7	—	.750	3.80	46	—	—	278	255	138	55
1921	Pitts.	NL	5	3	1	.625	2.98	10	4	1	48.1	45	19	13
1922	Pitts.	NL	3	1	0	.750	4.52	28	5	2	77.2	92	24	20
1923	Sacr.	PA	22	13	—	.629	3.68	57	—	19	311	351	99	79
1924	Sacr.	PA	1	4	—	.200	6.07	10	—	—	46	—	10	14
1924	Ft.Wth.	TL	NA											
1925	Mobile	SA	2	0	—	1.00	—	4	—	—	9.2	14	2	4
1925	Sacr.	PA	NA	(did not pitch)										
1926	Omha.	WL	NA											

MOSE YELLOWHORSE

Last known picture of YellowHorse as a professional
baseball player with Omaha, 1926

Courtesy of the Pawnee Annual Homecoming

Cartoons and Other Fantasies

"You know Mose was in the *Dick Tracy* comic strip."
—Anna Mulder, Pawnee elder

Part I: Other Fantasies

AFTER CLOSING OUT HIS PROFESSIONAL BASEBALL CAREER IN 1926 WITH the Omaha Royals, YellowHorse returned to the Pawnee tribal grounds, where, by most accounts, he took on odd jobs and began drinking with unfortunate proficiency. When talking to tribal members about YellowHorse's life between 1926 and 1945, they shared very little with me. As best I can tell, YellowHorse's day-to-day routine consisted of working both on the tribal grounds and in town, spending a good deal of time drinking, and playing lots of semipro baseball. Whatever the explanation for his drinking, it's clear that most people, both Pawnees and non-Indians, believed he had a drinking problem. Though it's fairly easy to speculate about the reasons why he started drinking more profusely after his professional baseball career ended, most of those reasons would be guesses. But it wouldn't seem that putting one's Chilocco-learned carpentry skills to use or working assorted jobs would be as stimulating as twirling fastballs at major league batters, certainly not as well-paying. The fact is, he endured a twenty-year drinking period. In the process, he may have had to come to terms with such facts:

1) in 1926, he was twenty-eight and both his parents were already dead,
2) Earl Kunz (the man for which Pittsburgh traded YellowHorse) had a shorter career than Mose,
3) Rabbit Maranville was not going to stop in for a visit,
4) Most of the money was gone,
5) His dad had sold his allotment land to H. E. Miller (in 1917),
6) Many people thought he had not performed to his potential.

This is, of course, a lot of disappointment for a twenty-eight-year-old to deal with. Unfortunately, YellowHorse dealt with it in the same way as many former professional athletes, which is to say through a haze.

The probability that YellowHorse remained in an unproductive stupor for twenty years, however, is slim. Although Yellowhorse consumed lots of alcohol and gained a reputation as a problem drinker, as many testimonies and stories suggest, he could not have consistently performed odd jobs and continued to stay with folks if he was always "in a state." Anna Mulder, among others, conveyed to me that YellowHorse regularly stayed with her, during both his drinking years and after he quit drinking, and cheerfully helped out with things around her house.

Though many people were disappointed that YellowHorse did not turn out to be the next Bender and held a grudge as a result, he did manage to keep a few close friends, including his half-brother, Ben Gover. Gover and Yellowhorse became drinking buddies and often sought out trouble—a result of restlessness.

Then, in 1945, he quit drinking, cold turkey. Exactly what event or epiphany caused YellowHorse to quit is not known or at least not discussed. Did he simply get tired of drinking or experience some painful and unsettling ramifications as a result of his behavior? Either way, he was happier because of it. As he later told a Sacramento newspaper in 1958, "Thirteen years ago I decided I'd give up drinking. I came to that decision on my own. And I did it with will power."[1]

YellowHorse's quitting allowed him to put a close to the most troubled period of his life and also to reconnect to his love of baseball. Afterward, he worked as an umpire in the Kansas-Oklahoma-Missouri League (KOM), as a groundskeeper for the Ponca City ball club, and as a coach for an all-Indian team. Near the end of his life he also worked as a foreman for the Oklahoma highway department. As well, he garnished numerous tributes from former baseball employers and admirers. These tributes and the opportunities that remained offered him a large degree of happiness and fulfillment.

Though YellowHorse was able to quit drinking and to find satisfaction with his life and routines, there occurred in the midst of this troubled period an odd tribute. A cartoon character based on YellowHorse appeared in the *Dick Tracy* comic strip. The character, Chief Yellowpony, appeared at a moment in YellowHorse's life when that moment least resembled the figure that has been passed on through the stories. The appearance of a cartoon character based on his likeness serves, in some ways, as a metaphor for the period he endured at the time of Yellowpony's arrival in the *Tracy* narrative.

Part II: And Cartoons

On March 28, 1935, in newspapers across the country a new character was introduced in the popular *Dick Tracy* comic strip. Named Chief Yellowpony, the character was based on YellowHorse, who was two years older than *Tracy* creator Chester Gould. The explanation for the character's appearance is quite simple, as Darrell Gambill, President of the Pawnee Chamber of Commerce points out: "Chester Gould put Pawnee-related material in his cartoon all the time. Storefronts and people, all kinds of stuff."[2] For Gould, it was a way of commemorating both the town in which he grew up and the people who lived there. Though Gould left Oklahoma in 1921, he kept childhood images of Pawnee close to his drawing pen, and so felt it appropriate to include various people and their surroundings in his strip.

Like Anna Mulder, other tribal members who told me about the appearance of the Yellowpony character often did so with smiles on their faces. I was given the impression quite clearly that most people thought the character rather funny—campy, even. This is because Gould's cartoon character bears little resemblance to YellowHorse, aside from a thick physical build. The obvious stereotypic depiction, a common occurrence with all of the strip's characters, should not come as a surprise when considering the 1930s context. What is somewhat surprising, given the plethora of

Indian stereotypes at the time (and even now), is that Yellowpony plays a hero's role almost from the time he's introduced into the strip. Unlike many other depictions of Indians as violent savages, Yellowpony plays a key role, as Gould gives the character intelligent and insightful attributes. He becomes a major character who helps in the capturing of two escaped criminals, Boris and Zora Arson. On March 28, 1935, Yellowpony makes his first appearance:

Courtesy of Tribune Media Services

And for the next two months Yellowpony is an everyday character in the strip.

Since YellowHorse and Gould were so close in age, it's no surprise to find that they could have been, and were, close friends.[3] Certainly Gould knew of YellowHorse's success as a professional baseball player. And in 1921, when YellowHorse was pitching for the Pirates in Pittsburgh, Gould left Oklahoma A & M College (now Oklahoma State University) and headed for Chicago. While Yellow-Horse found temporary prosperity playing ball, Gould struggled to make ends meet. He did manage to graduate from Northwestern in 1923. In 1924, when YellowHorse's arm finally went out on him, Gould gained full-time employment as a cartoonist for the syndicated strip *Fillum Fables.* Then, Gould developed *Dick Tracy* in 1931, and it first appeared on October 12.

Given that YellowHorse was in the midst of a tumultuous period in his life, it would seem reasonable to assume that Yel-lowHorse was indifferent to the appearance of the Yellowpony character in *Dick Tracy.* But according to both Becky Eppler, a Pawnee tribal member, and Gladys Kitchen, a volunteer at the Pawnee County Historical Society, that was not the case. Kitchen indicated that YellowHorse and Gould "were buddies" and that "Mose'd sometimes visit Chester in Woodstock, Illinois." Eppler stated that Mose "thought it [the appearance of Yellowpony] was funny" and that "it wasn't a big deal."[4] From both these views, it's easy to determine that YellowHorse wasn't disappointed about Gould's development of a character who, in more ways than not, bore little resemblance to himself. To see the appearance of a character based on his likeness must have been stimulating on one level.

The April 1 strip, entitled "Nice People," shows Gould's typical depiction of Yellowpony, Cottonflower, his wife, and Sunset, his daughter, throughout the narrative:

From this, and the first two strips in which the character speaks, it is obvious that the Yellowpony character more closely resembles popular, even romantic or noble depictions of Indians in the 1930s, rather than YellowHorse. That's one possible reason why numerous tribal members laugh at the character's traits. Through Gould, the Yellowpony character frequently makes use of the popular, though inaccurate, interjection "ugh," wears braids, lives in a teepee, etc. Given this, the closeness between Gould and YellowHorse, and Gould's understanding of the Pawnee tribe, I'm inclined to believe that Gould knew he was creating a character who held little in common with the real YellowHorse. The fact remains that Yellowpony, in the end, helps Tracy capture three criminals; he plays the role of a hero, without assimilating—a complex and confusing dynamic.

Like all characters in *Dick Tracy*, even the strip's leading man, the participants are rather flat. The very title suggests as much. Gould stated years later that he wanted Tracy to be "a strong representative of law and order who would take an eye for an eye and a tooth for a tooth," and he went on to explain that his motivation for creating the character came as a reaction against wide-spread "revelations [in the 1920s and 30s] of fixed juries, crooked judges, bribery of public officials and cops who looked the other way" (*Something about the Author* 113).[5] Such a character, one who lives in a black-and-white world of binaries (especially in the political and racial climate of the 1930s), has little choice but to interpret images of the world in reductive ways.

The *Tracy* narrative in which Yellowpony, his wife Cotton-flower, and daughter Sunset play central roles begins on March 27 and runs through May 22, some sixty daily episodes. Through the course of the story, Yellowpony is first introduced as a gullible character—formerly taken in by Boris Arson's con games. Over the course of the narrative, however, Yellowpony comes to recognize Boris Arson's sinister nature. At first he is prompted because of a phone call by Arson to drive himself and his family to the city, presumably Chicago, to have his daughter marry Arson. Thus begins, as it always does in the *Dick Tracy* strip, a series of harrowing and intense events involving Tracy, Pat Patton (Tracy's sidekick), Yellowpony, Cottonflower, Sunset, Boris and Zora Arson, and "Cutie" Diamond, another criminal with whom Arson and his sister hide out. With this, the overall plot progresses as a series of chance encounters, uncovering of schemes, and the pursuit of criminals.

By the time that Yellowpony reaches the apartment where Boris and Zora Arson are hiding, he has met Tracy and twice crashed his car. After Yellowpony and his family arrive at the Arsons' hideout, they are all enthusiastically welcomed by the escaped criminal, as the April 4th episode shows:

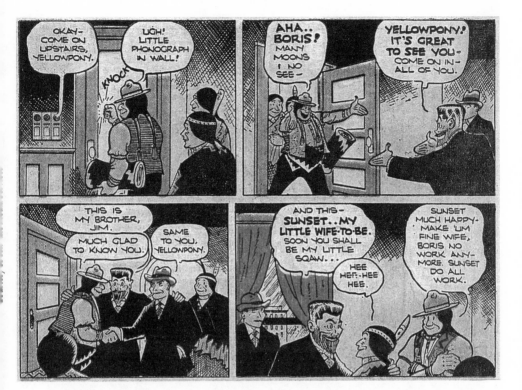

After this scene, Yellowpony insists (over and over) that the wedding take place immediately; Arson disagrees; the two men fight; and Yellowpony and his family are essentially kidnapped. Then, as the five of them attempt to flee the city in order to reach a hideout in Oklahoma, Yellowpony yells at an onlooking Tracy from the speeding car. As a result, Arson strikes Yellowpony on the head and then tumbles out of the car. Once Tracy and Pat Patton find Yellowpony and listen to the details of his story, the chase is on.

Then, through a series of clues (pieces of red fabric torn from Cottonflower's blanket), Yellowpony, Tracy, and Patton are able to follow Arson and Zora down to the hills of the Ozarks. On the way, however, Boris and Zora try to get rid of Cottonflower and Sunset by hiding them in lockers at an empty railroad station. After Yellowpony, Tracy, and Patton find the two women and get them safely aboard a train to Oklahoma, they begin their pursuit in earnest. And through another a series of clues, they are able to follow Boris and Zora to "Cutie" Diamond's mountain hideout. Diamond, the "King Bandit of the Southwest," welcomes the two crooks, and in the April 29 episode shows off some of his "trophies," which include a sheriff's badge he got in Hallet, Oklahoma, a bank teller's eye-shade that he took during a stick up near Little Rock, a police officer's cap that he snatched in a small town near Arkansas City, and a police officer's skull.

The crooks are not safe, however, as Yellowpony's abilities directly lead Tracy and Patton to the Arsons and "Cutie" Diamond's hideout.

And on May 4:

Once Yellowpony discovers the hideout and tells Tracy, it's only a matter of time before the crisis comes to a head. As Arson, Zora, and "Cutie" realize their situation, they decide to shoot their way out, and when they do, both Zora and "Cutie" are killed by gunfire. Boris, who retreats back into the cave with the initial burst of fire, is then shot and wounded by Tracy. Finally, in Yellowpony's final frame on May 22, he says his good-byes to Tracy and Pat Patton:

As the strip closes, Yellowpony offers his thoughts on the situation with stereotypical sage advice in an episode titled "Observations of an Indian." The observations he comes to are those shared by all the heroes involved in the *Dick Tracy* strip, a common punch line restated with every conclusion in the *Tracy* serial narratives.

For Gould, the *Tracy* strip and the lead character became intimately linked to his life, as much, say, as Charlie Brown became linked to Charles Schultz. The strip and all its commercial derivations earned Gould a comfortable living, and the strip, under different writership, continues to appear in newspapers across the country.

Notes

1   Bob Lemke, "Pirates Pitcher Went 'Way of all Bad Injuns,'" *The Bleacher Bum: Sports Collectors Digest*, 3 Mar. 1994.

2   Interview, 30 Mar. 1996.

3   Interview, 15 Mar. 2001.

4   Interview, 15 Mar. 2001.

5   I recognize that Gould often developed characters, including Tracy, who were wildly over-blown, caricatures most of the time, so that detectives, sympathetic characters, and gangsters all take on stereotypic traits. I would point out, however, that they all live in a contemporary world, while Yellowpony and his family seem caught in the nineteenth century.

Todd Fuller

Throat

"He hit her so hard in the throat that she couldn't talk for a
month."
                                        —Two Pawnee women, 1992

I T'S ONE STORY THAT FEW PEOPLE TALKED, OR TALK, ABOUT. IN FACT, WHEN
I tried to find confirmation from other tribal members that YellowHorse hit Beatrice Epple (his supposed wife), my questions
were most often met with looks of puzzlement. Nobody seemed to
know that YellowHorse was even married. Given this, none of the
elders would validate or deny the story.

So the narrative stands by itself and suggests a side of YellowHorse that is unseemly: I am left assuming that YellowHorse
the drinker becomes YellowHorse the wife beater. Here's the way it
could've happened: he's out drinking all night and comes home at
six or seven in the morning; she meets him at the door with questions and a strong dose of anger; then YellowHorse reacts by hitting
her in the throat; though seriously hurt by the blow, Beatrice Epple
has enough gumption to tell him to get the hell out.

Exactly when this might have occurred I am not certain since
the two women who told me did not give me a date. And their
identity is uncertain also. As soon as they told me the story, they
got up and left the dining hall. In my repeated attempts to find
them, I was unsuccessful; it was as though they had disappeared.
One of the women did tell me that Beatrice Epple was her great-
aunt.

The one assumption I feel fairly comfortable making about
this story is that it occurred during the twenty-year span of YellowHorse's heaviest drinking, between 1926 and 1945.

Throat, or the Demise of a Former Major Leaguer

It begins to unravel, first with a man stumbling
Through a front door at eight in the morning

And the stench of whiskey that steams from
Every pore. His skin damp from a three-week

Binge. Then there's the woman who meets his
First step into the house with a solemn glare.

Her words hurled at his ears like a high and tight
Fastball. And she says she's had it up to here,

Her right arm raised above her head. The sun
Casts the shadow of her body across the length

Of the living room, across the mantle, pictures
Of relatives. That's when the man's hand curls

Itself into a fist; that's when he raises it, throws
It across the room. At some point in midflight

It reaches the woman's throat. And the impact
Sounds like a baseball just before shattering

A window. That's when we should avert our eyes;
Look away from the arc of a blue vase breaking

Against a wall. Maybe we've seen too much
Already. Maybe the man's stunned expression, his

Standing over her in disbelief, is enough. It might
Be the woman's body twisting on the floor and her

Hands wrapped around her throat are enough.
When she rises to her feet, the man takes two

Steps back. He stares down the barrel of her
Index finger and cannot dodge the words climbing

From the back of her throat:
Out!
Out!

And when he leaves, and when she slams the door
After him, when a month has passed and she can

Speak without pain, all hints of his presence will be
Gone, not a stitch of baseball in the house.

. . .

Now when women (whether younger or older) speak of YellowHorse, they remember him as kind and gentle, as warm hearted
in his middle and old age. They say he never scared them in any
way, let alone hurt them. He was jovial and pleasant, respectful.

And maybe one reason the story about Beatrice Epple does not
get frequently told is out of a respect for both of their memories.

Some Tributes

Courtesy of John G. Hall

"MOSES YELLOWHORSE, Still Pitchin' on Diamond," 16 July 1947

The Chief ... came up to Ponca City this spring when he heard Brooklyn was establishing a Class D farm [team] here. Yellow Horse wanted a job as coach or umpire, assignments he had filled with semi-pro clubs since leaving Organized Ball in 1926. There were no such openings, Mose was told, but how about working as a groundskeeper in Ponca City's Conoco Park?

The 49-year-old Pawnee accepted with reluctance, disappointed he would not be able to show the youngsters how he whiffed 'em in the National League with his fast righthanded delivery.

Al Kaff, *The Sporting News*, 16 July 1947

Ironies Named 1947

"[Mose] Yellow Horse Hitches to Post of Ponca City
Groundskeeper"
　　　　　—Al Kaff, *The Sporting News*, 16 July 1947

One

It's an hour before game time on April 15,
And a man with a rake is smoothing

Infield dirt. And somewhere in the stands
A father will point him out, and a story

Will follow. The one about a Pawnee Indian
Striking out three future Hall of Famers

With nine undisguised fastballs, or maybe
The one about his beaning Ty Cobb right

Between the eyes. And the son will say
"Babe Ruth, really?" And the father will

Nod, then say other names like Gehrig
And Lazzeri. He'll tell his son, "Ol' Mose

Threw as hard as Walter 'Big Train' Johnson,"
And the boy will know that means

Over ninety miles per hour.

Two

In thirty minutes the Ponca City diamond
Is littered with spit-shined baseballs in flight,

And somewhere in Brooklyn, 26,000 fans
Watch Jackie Robinson break the color barrier

With an o-for premiere. And headlines in
Pittsburgh will be composed with Justice

In mind: *Triumph of Whole Race Seen
In Jackie's Debut.* And parents will name

Their newborns after him. And the citizens
Of Cairo, Georgia, are not surprised that

Little Jack Robinson's running like a damn
Gazelle around the bases. And half the fans

Jammed into Ebbets Field have a tear
For the moment. And someone's yelling

"Yonkel, Yonkel!" which is Yiddish
For Jackie.

Three

Boys in Ponca City, Oklahoma, will start
To fall asleep beside their radios, and they'll

Believe they saw a whale of a game
At Conoco Park, that the Oilers turned

Double plays just as slick as Reese to
Stanky to Robinson. And some announcer's

Voice will lull them into unconsciousness
With hyperbolic renditions of flying saucers

And alien landings. And Mose YellowHorse
Will return home four hours after the game

Is finished and settle his eyes onto an evening
Paper. There is talk of recently discovered

Biblical texts in Khirbet Qumran. In sports,
The Pirates and Dodgers won. In weather,

The hi-temp reached 56. Out on the porch
The wind carries smells of rain; the swing's

Creaking like an old tree branch.

Early this season, [YellowHorse] found
himself shaking hands with Brooklyn
Scout Andy High who played against the
Indian in the Southern Association and the
National League.
   "If he hadn't been pointed out, I wouldn't
have recognized the Chief," the one-time
St. Louis infielder said later, "but I'll never
forget what it meant to face that Indian
with a bat in your hand."
                    Al Kaff, *The Sporting News*, 16 July 1947

A partial list of Indians who played major league baseball before 1947:

Name	Tribe	M.L. Team	Years
Louis Sockalexis (of)	Penobscot	Cleveland (Spiders)	1897-99
Bill Phyle (p)	Lakota	Chic. (N), N.Y. (N), St. L.(N)	1898-99, 1901, 1906
Charles Bender (p)	Ojibwa	Phil. (A), Phil. (N), Chic. (A)	1903-17, 1925
Louis Bruce (of)	Mohawk	Phil. (A)	1904
Louis LeRoy (p)	Seneca	N.Y. (A), Bost. (A)	1906. 1908, 1910
Ed Summers (p)	Kickapoo	Det.	1908-12
John Meyers (c)	Cahuilla	N.Y. (N), Bklyn., Bost. (N)	1909-1917
George Johnson (p)	Winnebago	Cin., KC (F)	1913-15
Jim Thorpe (of)	Sac and Fox	N.Y. (N), Cin., Bost. (N)	1913-1919
Ben Tincup (p)	Cherokee	Phil. (N), Chic. (N)	1914-18, 1928
Jim Bluejacket (p)	Cherokee	Bklyn. (F), Cin. (N)	1914-16
Pepper Martin (of)	Osage	St. L. (N)	1928-44
Roy Johnson (3b)	Cherokee	Det., Bost. (A), N.Y. (A), Bost. (N)	1929-38
Bob Johnson (of)	Cherokee	Phil. (A), Wash., Bost. (A)	1933-45
Allie Reynolds (p)	Muscogee	Clev., NY (A)	1942-54

Other players also said to be Indian spent time in the majors. Because I could not find a tribal affiliation for these ballplayers, I did not include them in the list above. (This is not done out of disrespect to them, but rather because my research turned up no evidence.) They include Jim Toy, brothers Zack and Mack Wheat, Cal McLish, Rudy York, Elon Hogsett, Joe McGinnity, and Isaac Kahdot.

Baseball Gloves and Reconciliations

"His glove's in the Baseball Hall of Fame"
—Norman Rice, Pawnee tribal member

I N 1958, BOB MCKECHNIE, YELLOWHORSE'S FORMER MANAGER WITH THE Pirates donated one of YellowHorse's gloves to the Baseball Hall of Fame and Museum. That such an occurrence came to pass seems curious given the possible volatility of their relationship when they parted company in 1922 after the pigeon affair. I have yet to come across an account that explains the exact process of McKechnie's donating the glove to the Museum—no records in Cooperstown, no oral narratives.

. . .

In 1962, McKechnie was voted into the Hall of Fame.

. . .

The caption in the display case reads:
"Glove [worn by?] Moses 'Chief' YellowHorse, Pittsburgh Pirates, pitcher, [1921-22?]"

The Softening of Hard Feelings over Thirty-five Years

This is a story that begins with a letter
or phone call. Which is to say, it begins
before anyone's written or said a word.
Which is to say, it begins with someone's
desire to quiet a moment of remorse.
That's the way it usually is with healing,
unexpected thoughts about person x or y
implode within the body to the point of
agitation, until it's a need. And it could
be that three decades was long enough
for two men to hold "go to hell" against
the other. Maybe there was a reunion
in Florida. Maybe a conversation took
place, something that translated to "I'm
sorry." And somewhere along the way
a handshake was shared, some degree
of a smile crossed each man's older face.
And now there's a ball glove nestled in
a display case for forty years, a kind
of artifact in Cooperstown, New York.
And maybe it's no surprise that not
one Pawnee has ever seen it resting
in state, that no Pawnee children ever
slipped their left hands into the glove's
round palm or spit into its webbing.
It's no surprise that fathers in Pittsburgh
can tell their kids how everyone used
to yell "Bring in YellowHorse," & how
"Deacon" McKechnie led the Pirates
to the World Series in 1925. It's no
surprise that people learn to laugh at
the retellings of certain stories over

cups of coffee, like, say, the one about
eight angry pigeons flying for a man's
face in the middle of the night. How
they learn to laugh at old pain.

Hunting, for YellowHorse

A s MOSE YELLOWHORSE SETTLED INTO LATE MIDDLE AGE, HE CONTINUED
to hunt and fish religiously, same as when he was a kid. Many
Pawnee elders shared stories about the enjoyment he gained from
going out either to the woods or to a lake. In fact, when most tribal
members addressed this aspect of his life, a smile often crossed
their faces at some point. They seemed to take pride in the fact that
even as he got older, he remained physically fit and was able to
spend extended amounts of time out in the woods. Even non-
Pawnees like D Jo Ferguson, the longtime owner and publisher of
The Pawnee Chief, the town's newspaper, stated that YellowHorse
had the physique of a thirty-five-year-old into his sixties.[1] And
though most of the elders' accounts reinforce the fact that he liked
to hunt and fish, a couple of stories, it seems to me, move beyond
short statements of fact into a realm of myth making. Take this
story told by Pawnee John Jake:

> When Mose used to go hunting,
> he took two clubs
> and his dog
> into the woods, while
> other men took guns.
> It didn't matter,
> Mose 'd still come out
> of the woods
> with more rabbits
> than anyone.[2]

Such a story, which seemed to me at first as if it embraced just
as much imagination as fact, was told in the presence of another

tribal member, Norman Rice, who nodded with a straight face, as if
to confirm its validity. When I asked other tribal members if
YellowHorse hunted in such a way, they all responded with affirma-
tive answers: "He sure did," or "Oh, yeah, he hunted with a club."[3]

Shortly after hearing Jake's story, I imagined YellowHorse
emerging from a woods, dropping his club, and though exhausted,
pulling behind him the bodies of squirrels, rabbits, snakes, even
armadillos. I conjured in my mind the image of a sixty-something
YellowHorse returning from his hunt with enough booty to feed
Pawnees for a week. That's the way I wanted to see him: Yellow-
Horse the hunter doing his part to keep government-surplus food
off the table. I believed that upon his return a feast ensued. Tribal
members gathered to enjoy what YellowHorse brought them. They
thanked him, gave him smiles and slaps on the back. Songs
emerged from the satisfied mouths of mothers and fathers. The
radio played a baseball game, maybe the Pirates defeating the Yankees 6 to 4 in the first game of the 1960 World Series. And children
strained to listen to YellowHorse tell stories about Ruth, Gehrig,
and Cobb; they turned to their parents and said, "He mowed 'em all
down?" I wanted to believe that the telling of stories went on well
into the night, that the moment commemorated all YellowHorse
had done: helping support his parents from the get-go (first by performing in Pawnee Bill's Wild West Show, then by bringing home
food), leading the baseball teams at Chilocco Indian School and Little Rock to championship seasons, and pitching for a couple of
strong Pittsburgh teams in the early 1920s. All these things and
more remembered by YellowHorse and other Pawnee members.
That's how it would have been. Lots of lip smacking and belly rub-
bing. Then there'd be more of the same the next day (and night)
and the next day, too, for a whole week—a feast for all who
wanted. That's how I imagine YellowHorse's return from hunting
with a club.

Of course, YellowHorse did share many of the rabbits and squirrels he'd bagged with friends like Nora Pratt's family, Anna
Mulder's husband and kids, and Earl Chapman's family. Whether

or not a party commenced when YellowHorse returned from a hunt is anyone's guess. What's certain is the enjoyment he took from outdoor recreational sports. Earl Chapman shared that:

> Mose enjoyed fishing, too.
> He liked to fish at Fork Kitchen Pond.
> We used to go out together
> and spend hours.
>
> A week before he died
> we went out there together
> and he caught a five-pound bass.[4]

After telling this story, Mr. Chapman, who was confined to a wheelchair after suffering a stroke, started to tear up. He seemed to look past me and quickly, barely shook his head.

· · ·

Joseph Oxendine reports in *American Indian Sports Heritage,* "In 1876 Big Hawk Chief, a Pawnee Indian, ran the world's first recorded sub-four-minute mile at the Sidney barracks in Nebraska. Though this race was timed by two army officers with stop watches and the track was later meticulously measured with a steel tape, it remains unofficial"(163). In *The Pawnee Indians,* George Hyde tells a story dating back to 1875:

> The people were so hungry and so eager to hunt that the chiefs kept young warriors stationed at Fort Reno, 100 miles west of the Pawnee agency, to report promptly if herds of buffalo appeared in that district, the only one in which the Pawnees were permitted to hunt. On one occasion two Pawnee buffalo scouts at Fort Reno, White Eagle (David Gillingham) and Dog Chief (Simon Adams) went on foot, running most of the way, from the post to the Pawnee agency, 96 miles, between early morning and evening on the same day, to report the presence of buffalo. (334)

These two stories, along with those told about YellowHorse, demonstrate not only admirable physical strength but great endurance. In the case of YellowHorse, the narratives told of him can be thought of as declarations of one individual's resiliency, which in turn reflects the resiliency and tenacity of the whole Pawnee tribe. With YellowHorse, it's easy to identify specific examples of his fortitude. Consider that he made the team at Chilocco his first year there, despite having never played organized ball; that in Little Rock in 1920, he contracted the flu in the middle of the season, and then after regaining his health didn't lose a game the rest of the year; that in 1921, while trying out with Pittsburgh, he earned a spot on the pitching staff, though everyone was surprised that the Pirates even invited him to their spring training camp. All these experiences demonstrate that YellowHorse was a determined man, who consistently overcame long odds, surpassed the expectations of those around him.

As for the story told by John Jake about YellowHorse's hunting prowess, like many stories regarding outstanding individual physical feats that seem to stretch the boundaries of probability, it must be remembered that Native American oral histories are, as scholars Devon Mihesuah and Paula Gunn Allen argue, a valid (and vibrant) means of understanding a particular tribal culture. Stories like Jake's, which might seem far-fetched to white scholars, ought to be taken as historical documents. It's quite a compliment to YellowHorse that elders and other tribal members remember so many specific stories about him more than a generation after his death. It is, after all, an expression of joy, the imagination and memory intermingling.

Notes

1 From a letter Ferguson wrote on 2 May 1964 to Lee Allen, then curator at the Baseball Hall of Fame and Museum.

2 Jake shared this story with me on 17 June 1992.

3 Both Earl Chapman and Phil Gover confirmed that YellowHorse hunted with a club.

4 Earl Chapman told this story to me on 18 June 1992. (I should say, too, that I am well aware of the possibility of a kind of "rite-of-passage" tradition that occurs at the expense of outsiders, often white scholars, who conduct field studies with various tribal communities. It is not uncommon for tribal members to share stories that are more fanciful and creative in nature, which sometimes leads to work that seems improbable.)

A Curveball Story

—As told by Phil Gover, Pawnee elder, 16 June 1992

"**I** REMEMBER THIS ONE ABOUT MOSE.

"It must've been in the late 50s or early 60s, so Mose was getting older. But he was still in great shape. This one day he's in town throwing a ball around with some kids. And they're having fun. You know, Mose remembering how it was, and the kids dreaming how it could be. Then one of the older guys in town, one of the town's leaders, saw him playing catch with these kids. And this guy comes over and crouches behind the kid who's catching Mose. He watches Mose throw a couple pitches, and he says to Mose, 'I bet you still can't throw a curve.'

"Mose says, 'Okay, you catch me and see if I can't throw a curve.'

"The guy took the kid's mitt and said to Mose, 'Go ahead. Fire away.'

"Mose made the first one real easy, just a fastball. He took a little off of it, but the guy still took off the glove and rubbed and shook his left hand 'til he could feel it again. Mose gives the guy another soft pitch, then tells him 'Here's my curve.' And he rages back and fires it, throws the guy his best curve. The guy raises the mitt, expecting like it's coming straight at his mitt. He thinks it's a wild pitch or something. Then all of a sudden, the ball breaks real sharp; it breaks two feet and hits the guy right in the throat. He falls over, grabbing his throat and trying to breathe, lying there just rolling on the ground. And all the kids, and Mose, are standing over him and smiling. No one says a word. They just smile. And Mose told the guy, 'I haven't thrown a curve in years.'

"It was the same guy who didn't want Mose to head up the new Little League in Pawnee."

Ghost Dancing in January:
A Transcript and Character Profile

FROM JUNE 1992 TO JUNE 1999, I'M SURE I SPOKE TO OVER A HUNdred Pawnee tribal members about YellowHorse. In those seven years, only two people spoke badly of YellowHorse, cast him as an indecent character. Every other person, from the eldest elder to young people in their twenties, spoke of YellowHorse in rather glowing terms. When considering YellowHorse's role as an elder and leader in the Pawnee community in the 1950s and '60s, it became clear that he was an important and vital member. Not only did he bring a certain amount of celebrity status to the tribe (because of all the baseball-related tributes held in his honor in places like Sacramento and Pittsburgh), he also was a keeper of the culture: he knew ghost dance songs, how to play hand games, the importance of various ceremonies (including the pipe ceremony, the cedar ceremony, the corn ceremony), and the steps to numerous dances. On January 25, 1964, less than three months before YellowHorse died on April 10, the tribe held a celebration in his honor. One estimate has it that over 700 attended the function, which involved both afternoon and evening sessions of dancing, singing, playing hand games, and performing ceremonies.

Anthropologist Martha Royce Blaine, who married Pawnee tribal member Garland Blaine and wrote several books on the Pawnees, including *Pawnee Passage: 1870-1875*, *The Pawnees: A Critical Bibliography*, and *Some Things Are Not Forgotten: A Pawnee Family Remembers*, sat behind YellowHorse during the celebration to record his reactions and thoughts on the day's events. One recorded passage in particular stands out, a speech he made during the evening dance session. What follows is Martha Royce Blaine's transcript of the tape of YellowHorse's speech.

He said:

I wish to say a word or two. During this day, early this morning, during the day, I have been reverent, happy. You have made me feel that way. The way things have gone with your help and cooperation, I am very thankful, very happy. You have made me happy. This was your dance, your gathering. I was glad to see each and every one of you take part. When I go home, I will remember every one of you in my prayers.

There was a request through a letter from my friend, Sam Gordon [owner of the Sacramento baseball team]. He knew that this [dance] was to be today. In that letter, he said he wanted to know exactly the number of people that come [to the dance]. I would like to know how many people approximately in the tribe will have the celebration there. We know that there will be people there who will come there in happiness and joy [tape is unclear]. You have made me this way. The good is just now coming out [tape is unclear].

While I was sitting around and watching you people, I asked God. You contribute that food to nourish and strengthen your bodies. Sam Gordon, a very good friend of mine, has got every word spoken here in Sacramento. It is wonderful how things are being sent over there by telegraph. Someway, somehow, I don't know.

I am very happy. I am overjoyed to see each and every one of you take part in [this], and the food especially. It was your day. And what enjoyment it has been in thinking about everyone taking part in the dance, and enjoying yourself. Someday, I will see you back again, right here [background noise drowns out much of speech]. To your parents, I hope God answers every one of your prayers. Someday, everyone of you come back. When you go home, I hope you find things just like you left them. If there is any sickness, or sad feeling, I hope the Lord destroys that. I want to thank each and every one of you again. You don't know how happy I am. [A few inaudible last words before he finishes.]

· · ·

This speech and other comments he made during the dance make clear that YellowHorse had an exhaustive knowledge of his Pawnee culture—a knowledge in which he delighted: he knew his dad's ghost dance song and was, in fact, the only person who knew it until he taught the singers.

More than anything else, YellowHorse's speech, taken together with other comments he made during his dance, illuminates a significant aspect of his character: namely, how much pleasure he took in celebrating his Pawnee culture and heritage. In fact, as he matured from a cocky young ballplayer into a middle-aged, problem-drinking vagabond to an older, nondrinking, regularly employed state worker for the Oklahoma State Highway Department, YellowHorse was thought of by other tribal members as an important and well-liked leader in the community.

Take part of this speech delivered during YellowHorse's dance by Ben Gover (Goose), YellowHorse's half-brother:

> My friends, relatives and all, today my brother, Moses Yel-lowHorse, is celebrating his birthday.... I know he is happy, as well as I am, to see you people here to honor him with your presence. It is indeed inspiring to see so many people here enjoying themselves at the dance, and [with] the old ceremonies.... I am sure that my brother is happy today, that he is able to be here with us. He has been sick, and with his eyes he could not see for a while [as a result of his diabetes], but now he is back with us, and enjoying life, and I hope he will continue to enjoy that life again. We ask God to help him along the road, give him strength and courage to withstand all things that go against him in the experience of love. As I have said before, he loves each and every one of you. He's glad you are here.... [Remember too, that] kind words cost nothing. Kind words never die. They exist forever. When you speak to mankind, speak kind, and think of the joy you have given him by saying nice things about him. Do not intrude into other people's affairs. That is my brother's wish. Let us all continue one way, God's way. And I will say this, my brother and I wish the words of our mouths and the meditations of our hearts be acceptable with our Lord, Jesus.... And last, but not least, till we meet again, my brother and I wish you happy 1964. Until we meet again, may God bless you and keep you in His care.

. . .

The tenor of Ben Gover's words, the respect offered YellowHorse, is repeated by tribal members to this day. Those who knew him personally when they were younger now describe the older YellowHorse as a fun-loving storyteller, even a little long-winded, and as one who loved kids and treated people with respect. Despite his ill health in January of 1964, YellowHorse was determined to enjoy himself at his celebration—even to the point of dancing, which, according to many, he did little of.

Henry Stone Road, a tribal elder and 79 when I wrote this, told me that YellowHorse often spoke to him about ways he ought to behave. YellowHorse would advise Stone Road in their Pawnee language: "Don't make the same mistakes I made as a young man." Such advice, it seems, may have alluded in part to YellowHorse's drinking habit.[1] According to Stone Road, YellowHorse counseled many young Pawnee men to carry out their lives in a responsible manner, to be true to their Pawnee heritage first, and to pursue personal achievements second. Even as YellowHorse recognized the end of his life nearing, he reveled more in the celebration of tribal ceremonies than in his own baseball past.

That tribal elders continue to identify YellowHorse as kind and generous should come as no surprise, given the fact that tribal members could see that his concern for both the young people and the Pawnee culture was always genuine.

. . .

Notes

1   Apparently, YellowHorse started drinking again, right at the end of his life. This assertion derives from Martha Blaine's field notes of February and March, 1964. Some other people I spoke to could neither confirm nor deny Blaine's claim, though I was surprised to hear of this.

Some Conclusions

One of the last known pictures of YellowHorse.
On the back it says "April 1964."

Anna Mulder said of YellowHorse in 1992:

"He used to walk all over the place,
and people could hear him coming.
They knew he was coming by his whistle.
He could whistle the prettiest songs."

1964: The Day They Demolished the Polo Grounds, or Riding off into the Sunset (on April 10)

America cannot begin again,
but if it could there might be
star-spangled arrows aimed

at the Atlantic. & there might
be a spread of a thousand
feasts and a ball game after-

wards. All skinny as feathers:
smiling feather boys, smiling
feather girls, & songs nearly

twirling off sunbeams. It's a lie
worth believing now, after all
this time of war, warring, and

wars. No matter how we try,
our imaginations can't stop
anyone from dying alone. I'd

like to believe someone's hand
on his arm, an arrangement
from one of the boys. There's

a nurse who enters with a glass
of water and a card beside the
bed. She says something like:

Mornin', Mose, and smiles at
the song playing in her head,
something about, *I wanna hold*

your hand.

Obits and Other Fibs

On April 10, 1964, Mose YellowHorse died of an apparent heart attack, a heart ailment of some kind, probably in combination with diabetes. Apparently he was alone. Apparently he was alone in the hospital.

. . .

Shortly after he died, obituaries appeared in newspapers across Oklahoma and across the country. Including, among others, this one:

Chief YellowHorse, 66
Ex-Major Leaguer, Is Dead

PAWNEE—Chief Mose Yellowhorse has pitched his last inning.

He died Friday at the Pawnee hospital of a heart ailment.

Chief YellowHorse was said to be the first full-blood American Indian to play baseball in the major leagues.

Mose had lived in Stillwater at 125 S. Perkins Road while working for the State Highway Department. He retired from the department recently and returned to Pawnee.

In January, he celebrated his 66th birthday with a feast and dance for his Pawnee tribesmen. A special song was written in his honor and he was named "Fox Warrior" at the celebration.

He had been ill with a heart condition for some time and recently had been in the hospital for treatment. He was released from the hospital last week, but suffered another heart attack and was readmitted Friday.

Mose is survived only by a half-brother, Ben Gover, of Pawnee.

Funeral services were conducted at the Poteet Funeral Home and burial was in the North Indian Cemetery.

The Stillwater News Press, 17 April 1964

Obituary
Moses Yellow Horse

Moses (Chief) Yellow Horse, one of the few full-blooded Indians who reached the majors, died of an apparent heart attack at his home [sic] in Pawnee, Okla., April 10. He was 64 [sic].

The Sporting News

MOSE YELLOWHORSE

A proud Pawnee, Mose called Pawnee his home and was regularly employed by the State Highway Department for many years after his retirement from baseball. He passed away on April 10, 1964.

Unattributed

YELLOWHORSE,
FIRST FULL INDIAN
IN MAJORS, DIES

PAWNEE, OKLA., (AP).—Moses YellowHorse, who built his throwing arm hurling rocks at small animals and claimed to be the first full-blooded Indian to have played major league baseball, is dead.

Old-Time Pitcher
YellowHorse Dies

Pawnee—Mose Yellowhorse, 64, [sic] who broke into the major leagues as a 21-year-old rookie [sic] in 1921, died Friday night of an apparent heart attack.

Unattributed

**Moses Yellow Horse, famed Indian
athlete of other days, is dead**

Pawnee's most famous athlete, Moses Yellow Horse, passed away
Friday, April 10, and funeral services were held on Monday with
burial in the North Indian Cemetery. The tribe's mourning feast
was held on Tuesday.

Chief Yellow Horse, a name revered in baseball circles from
Pawnee to Little Rock to Sacramento and to Pittsburgh, was the
first full blood Indian to enter the major leagues. He pitched for
the Pirates in 1921-22, but an arm injury retired him after that.

His name was even eulogized by another of Pawnee's famous
sons, Chester Gould in his nation-wide comic strip, *Dick Tracy*, in
which he used the name Chief Yellow Pony.

The Pawnee Chief, 16 April 1964

. . .

And the one perpetual obituary is his headstone in North
Indian Cemetery in Pawnee. Anna Mulder was the one responsible
for the headstone. She said she decided on the epitaph because
"Mose had to be commemorated some way, and the stone was the
best way to do it."

Truth Is

A Pawnee died.
But I don't know
how many people sent
telegrams to Pawnee
when his obit appeared.
I don't know who
took his dog,
named Sissy.
I don't know if
his deathbed thoughts
included spring training.
I don't know if
his right arm raised itself
toward Pittsburgh.
I don't know if
the other raised
toward Nebraska.
I'll never know how
his voice wrapped itself
around a story.
But I'd like to think
he took pleasure in
reading box scores
and listening to
ghost dance songs.
I'd like to think
he was a hand game
master. I'd like
to imagine a moment
of silence was observed
in Pittsburgh, Sacramento,
and Little Rock.
I don't know how
many cigarettes he smoked

a day, or what kind.
I don't know if he died
in love or anger.
I don't know
which spirits guided him
away; if the voices
of his mother and father
greeted him. I don't
know if he ever owned
a palomino or named her
Fastball.
Truth is, I don't know
if he ever wanted kids,
or if there might be un-
accounted relatives
somewhere.
I don't know how many
major league baseballs
he kept in his house.
But I'd like to imagine
he kept a few souvenirs
stashed in a closet.
I'd like to consider
his 23-year-old body
walking to Forbes Field
every summer day.
I'd like a cup of coffee
and a piece of strawberry pie.
I'd like to imagine
the moment of his curve-
ball breaking over the plate.
The memory of a pitch
speeding across
Pawnee.

Posthumous Fastballs, Threats, and Chants

AWHILE BACK, AFTER VISITING SOME FOLKS IN PAWNEE, I WAS RETURN-
ing to Stillwater (some thirty miles away). As I drove along, I
admired the "Oklahoma foothills of the Ozarks," as Chester Gould
referred to them in his *Dick Tracy* strip in March 1935, and took in
the texture of the land that YellowHorse looked at every day of his
later life. I scanned the green hills and looked at houses built a
hundred feet from the road. I began to think about the accolades
YellowHorse received after he died, his induction into both the
Oklahoma Sports Hall of Fame (1971) and the American Indian
Athletic Hall of Fame (1994). It made me sad for a second to consider how happy YellowHorse would have been to receive these
affirmations during his lifetime. And he would have been
(humbly) pleased to see a ball field named in his honor built on the
tribal grounds, right next to the roundhouse. While these thoughts
helped me pass the time, I continued to look at assorted sights, like
the Pawnee Pipe Company, on my way out of town. As I came upon
a ranch entrance, I saw a sign that made me think about YellowHorse's role as a relief pitcher with the Pirates. It said:

DANGER

Bull Pen

Do Not Provoke

And I smiled again. I heard, for an instant, the fans in Pittsburgh, the many thousands, chanting one of their long-time
favorites: "Bring in YellowHorse! Bring in YellowHorse!"

Afterword

An Open Letter:
To the Baseball Hall of Fame Veterans' Committee

Dear Members of the Committee:

I am writing to nominate Mose YellowHorse for induction into the Baseball Hall of Fame.

I am writing because hardly anyone knows that the annual passage of spring training derives from an old-time Pawnee ritual.

I make this plea because Mose YellowHorse's Indian name was Fox Warrior, and because he had a better winning percentage than Cy Young.

I submit to you the facts and ask you to consider them for yourselves. He had fewer losses than Tom Seaver and is the only Indian in history to bean Ty Cobb, which must be worth a hundred votes.

I write because there are kids in Pawnee, Oklahoma, who live on Mose YellowHorse Drive, and also because he posted a better earned-run average in 1921 than Grover Cleveland Alexander.

But, as you know, baseball does not live on statistics alone.

So I ask that you consider that YellowHorse is the only major league player to appear in *Dick Tracy*, which is certainly in the Comic Strip Hall of Fame.

Consider also that he pitched at Chilocco Indian School, where he posted a perfect record in 1917 of 17-0. I write because the school was formerly a drug rehabilitation center.

Know too that YellowHorse won more games in his rookie season than Dizzy Dean, and Dean was elected to the Hall of Fame partly because of unrealized potential.

I ask you, then, if you induct only those players with the most impressive numbers?

I wonder if those who showed a love for the game during the span of a lifetime belong? Because in 1947 YellowHorse was a groundskeeper for a Brooklyn Dodger affiliate in Ponca City, Oklahoma, and you all know about broken color barriers in 1947.

And YellowHorse in 1950 coached an all-Indian baseball team that whipped half the minor league organizations in the Southern Association.

But you might not know that in 1958 his glove was inducted into the Baseball Hall of Fame and Museum. And if the glove belongs, then certainly the body of the left hand that fielded with the glove belongs in the Hall of Fame, too.

I am writing because after nearly a decade of studying Yellow-Horse I can say with complete certainty that few major leaguers (aside from the likes of Mickey Mantle and Ted Williams) are as celebrated in their hometowns as YellowHorse. You won't see it in gaudy signs along the highway, but you'll hear it in the stories told by those who knew him.

Members of the Veterans' Committee, I ask that you consider YellowHorse's induction because he caught pigeons bare handed with Hall of Famer Rabbit Maranville from a sixteenth-story hotel room in New York.

I submit this proposal to you because twenty-five years after he played in Pittsburgh the fans still yelled "Bring in YellowHorse!" when they wanted a dependable reliever on the mound. And that's cultural impact worth at least two hundred votes.

I write because former St. Louis Cardinal infielder Andy High said of YellowHorse, "I'll never forget what it meant to face that Indian with a bat in your hand." And there's a whole volume of race relations inherent in his words.

Finally, I ask that YellowHorse be inducted into the Hall of Fame because there's a ball field on the Pawnee tribal grounds dedicated to his memory, and it's going to save some lives over the next ten years.

I humbly thank you, members of the Veterans' Committee, for your attention in this matter. I shall look forward to the possibility of seeing a bronze bust of Mose YellowHorse in Cooperstown.

Moses YellowHorse Memorial Field, Pawnee, Oklahoma

Bibliography

First Meetings and Introductions
Churchill, Ward, Norbert S. Hill, Jr., Mary Jo Barlow. "An Historical Overview of Twentieth Century Native American Athletics." *The Indian Historian* 12.4 (1982): 22-32.

Lieb, Frank. *The Pittsburgh Pirates*. New York: Putnam's, 1948.

Ritter, Lawrence S. *The Glory of Their Times: The Story of the Early Days of Baseball Told by the Men Who Played It*. New York: Morrow, 1966.

Vila, Joe. "Chief YellowHorse Is Indian Pitcher." *The Sporting News* 20 Apr. 1921.

Considering Contexts: A Moment of Pawnee
Ballentine, Betty and Ian, eds. *The Native Americans: An Illustrated History*. Atlanta: Turner, 1993.

"History" ‹www.pawneenation.org.› 6 Oct. 1999.

"Space Talk: Pawnee Sky Observations" ‹hoa.aavso.org/spacetalk.htm› 27 July 2000.

Wright, Muriel H. *A Guide to the Indian Tribes of Oklahoma*. Norman: U of Oklahoma P, 1951.

A Dancing Red Spine and Other Convergences
Allen, Paula Gunn. "The Sacred Hoop." *Studies in American Indian Literature: Critical Essays and Course Design*. New York: MLA, 1983.

Chapman, Earl. Personal Interview. 18 June 1992.

Conlin, Bill. Personal Interview. 17 Sept. 1992.

Gover, Mariah. Personal Interview. 3 Mar. 1998.

Kaff, Al. "Yellow Horse Hitches to Post of Ponca City Groundskeeper." *The Sporting News* 16 July 1947: 42.

Hyde, George. *The Pawnee Indians*. Norman: U of Oklahoma P, 1974.

Kobler, John. *Ardent Spirits*. New York: Putnam, 1973.

Lieb, Frederick G. *The Pittsburgh Pirates*. New York: Putnam, 1948.

Mulder, Anna. Personal Interview. 19 June 1992.

Parks, Douglas. Introduction. *The Pawnee Mythology*. By George Dorsey. Lincoln: U of Nebraska P, 1997.

"Pirates Winners after Long Battle." *New York Times* 17 June 1921, late ed.: 35.

Rice, Norman. Personal Interview. 20 June 1992.

Cartoons and Other Fantasies
Suggested Readings

Barker, Martin. *Comics: Ideology, Power, and the Critics.* Manchester, Eng.: Manchester UP, 1989.

Berkhofer, Robert F. *The White Man's Indian.* New York: Knopf, 1978.

Hirschfelder, Arlene B. *American Indian Stereotypes in the World of Children: A Reader and Bibliography.* Metuchen, NJ: Scarecrow, 1982.

McNickle, D'Arcy. "American Indians Who Never Were." *The Indian Historian* 3 (1970): 4-7.

Mihesuah, Devon A. *American Indians: Stereotypes & Realities.* Atlanta: Clarity, 1996.

Stedman, Raymond William. *Shadows of the Indians: Stereotypes in American Culture.* Norman: U of Oklahoma P, 1982.

Hunting, for YellowHorse

Allen, Paula Gunn. "The Sacred Hoop." *Studies in American Indian Literature: Critical Essays and Course Design.* New York: MLA. 1983.

Hyde, George E. *The Pawnee Indians.* Norman: U of Oklahoma P, 1974.

Mihesuah, Devon A. *Natives and Academics: Researching and Writing About American Indians.* Lincoln: U of Nebraska P, 1998.

Oxendine, Joseph B. *American Indian Sports Heritage.* Lincoln: U of Nebraska P, 1988.

Ghost Dancing in January: A Transcript and Character Profile

Stone Road, Henry. Personal Interview. 11 May 1999.

Publication Credits

Some of the pieces in this book have previously appeared in the following journals:

American Indian Culture and Research Journal: "Memorizing Oklahoma,"
    "Wild West Shows and Other Histories,"
    "Picking Moments"
Crazyhorse: "Of All Things Winter"
Puerto del Sol: "A Dancing Red Spine, and Other Convergences: Mose
    YellowHorse, a Pawnee's (Baseball) Life"
Quarterly West: "An Open Letter: to the Baseball Hall of Fame Veterans'
    Committee"
South Dakota Review: "How to Read a Population Table." Also published in
    the composition textbook *The Great Plains: A Cross-Disciplinary Reader*
Weber Studies: Voices and Viewpoints of the Contemporary West: "The Way
    Mose YellowHorse Learned How to Throw along Black Bear Creek in
    Pawnee, Oklahoma before He Discovered the Meaning of a Fastball or
    Whistling,"
    "Something Pastoral (in 1917),"
    "What It Means to Wear #50 (for the Pittsburgh Pirates),"
    "Eight to Five,"
    "A Bean for the (Georgia) Peach,"
    "A Bean for the Peach: Counting Coup,"
    "Ironies Named 1947"

About the Author

Todd Fuller was born in Tacoma, Washington, on an air force base. He was raised in central Indiana and later worked at a book manufacturing company. After completing degrees in literature and creative writing at Indiana University and Wichita State University, he graduated with his Ph.D. in creative writing and Native American literatures and languages from Oklahoma State University. Since then, he has taught courses for the Pawnee Nation and at Northern Oklahoma College, and Drake University. His work has appeared in such journals as the *American Literary Review, Hawai'i Review, Poet Lore, Spoon River Poetry Review, Southwestern American Literature, Third Coast,* and *The William and Mary Review,* in addition to those journals that published pieces from this text. His work has earned him an Academy of American Poets Prize, a Poetry Fellowship at Wichita State University, and an award from the Indiana Collegiate Press Association. Though he lives in Iowa, he is a frequent traveler back to Oklahoma, where he continues to discover beautiful surprises in the landscape.

Half of the royalties from the sale of this book will help establish the Mose YellowHorse Endowment of Higher Education for Pawnee tribal members.